THE
DOLLHOUSE
DECORATOR

THE
DOLLHOUSE
DECORATOR

VIVIENNE
BOULTON

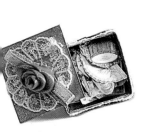

DK

DORLING KINDERSLEY, INC.

LONDON · NEW YORK · STUTTGART

Dedicated to Ella Waters, my grandmother

The Dollhouse Decorator
is a
CARROLL & BROWN
original creation

ART DIRECTION
Denise Brown   Lyndel Donaldson

EDITORIAL
Amy Carroll

PHOTOGRAPHY
David Murray   Jules Selmes

PRODUCTION CONSULTANT
Lorraine Baird

TYPESETTING
Rowena Feeny

Copyright © 1992

Carroll & Brown Limited
5 Lonsdale Road, London NW6

First American Edition, 1992
10 9 8 7 6 5 4 3 2 1
Published in the United States by
Dorling Kindersley, Inc., 232 Madison Avenue
New York, New York 10016

Boulton, Vivienne

Dollhouse Decorator / Vivienne Boulton, - 1st American ed.

p. cm.

ISBN 1-56458-077-6

1. Doll Furniture. I Title.   92-16014
                                      CIP
TT175.5.B68 1992

745.592'3-dc20

Reproduced by Colourscan, Singapore
Printed in Singapore by Tien Wah Press

CONTENTS

INTRODUCTION 6

WORKING WITH

PAPER AND CARD 8   CLAY/MODELING MEDIUM 10   WOOD 12

FABRICS 14   PAINT 16   BITS AND PIECES 17

KITCHENS

BEDROOMS

BATHROOMS

LIVING ROOMS

$\mathcal{I}$NTRODUCTION

Welcome to a world of dollhouse decoration that uses only readily available, inexpensive materials. Peruse the pages of this book and you will find a multitude of useful and attractive items to suit every doll's taste and needs. Though its scale may be small, the range of dollhouse furnishings that can be created is limited only by your imagination.

Dollhouse decoration as practiced in this book depends upon the mastery of a few simple techniques applied to materials that are inexpensive and easy to acquire. Furniture for the most part is made of wood strip and cardboard, while smaller accessories are created from clay and plastic modeling materials.

Paper and fabric, too, are essential for many household items and soft furnishings.

Immediately following this introduction is a section on the materials and techniques required for doll-house decorating. Not only will you learn how to transform plain card and wood into elaborately finished furnishings but you will begin to see how buttons, beads, and found objects can be transmuted into picture frames, bottles, and feather dusters.

Soon practically everything you see will acquire decorative possibilities.

A dollhouse can be decorated in any period style but the Victorian era is popular with the majority of dollhouse owners, and its rather overstuffed look provides scope for an enormous number of items. So although most of the rooms inside relate to Victorian times, several other styles are represented including Colonial, Art Deco, Country, and Contemporary.

All the major rooms in a house have been considered. There are kitchens, bedrooms–for adults and children, living rooms, and bathrooms.

Each one can be recreated to fit your dollhouse or even a decorated box. As well as the furniture, each room comes complete with furnishings, accessories, decorative items, and the normal paraphernalia of everyday life – then and now. Everything has play value, too, and a selection of small items can provide a child with hours of creative activity – both in the making and in the using.

Selected items of furniture are photographed separately and come with full making-up instructions and templates. Tables, chairs, beds, wardrobes, cupboards, and washstands are among the items covered. Their instructions and templates are found in the back of the book. Templates should never be cut out but should always be traced over and transferred to the recommended materials.

Other pieces of furniture are variations of the major items and for them, extended captions give making-up directions and, if necessary, advice on adapting particular templates.

Most of the smaller items contained in the rooms are displayed on catalog pages. Here you get to see hundreds of items up close, and are given instructions on how they are made. The range of accessories is enormous and includes crockery, cookware, food, clothing, soft furnishings, wall decorations, toys, jewelry, paper goods, linens, plants, boxes, and books.

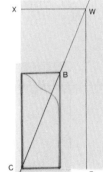
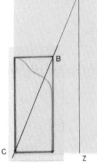

Finally, a dollhouse must be a home. Whose home it is falls within the abilities of a dollhouse decorator– particularly as complete how-to instructions on creating and clothing the family of your choice are included. Again, a few simple materials can bring to life a cast of thousands.

So be prepared to be entertained, astonished, and inspired. Let the dollhouse decorating begin!

WORKING WITH
*P*APER AND *C*ARD

Paper products are the most versatile and widely available of all craft materials. Every kind of paper and paper product is useable – from specially constructed art board through to wrapping paper, printed illustrations, decorative boxes, tissue paper, and toilet paper! Start saving your scraps; they are certain to be put to good use.

Cutting tools include scissors and a craft knife for cardboard

Sugar paper (center and right) can be effective as picture mounts, blotters and book jackets

Glue should be an all-purpose clear, strong adhesive (UHU); glue sticks are handy also

Foil (left) is used for "mirrors" and gift wrapping. It can be bought in sheets or as adhesive-backed plastic, or taken from candy wrappers and wine bottles. Kitchen foil can be used also

Shapes and rulers are useful for creating curved and geometric items

Wrapping paper is used to cover walls and boxes

Tissue paper is used as the real thing and for creating fires

Masking tape is used to rough assemble pieces, and for hinges and plants

Tape is used for joins; transparent tape is handy when an invisible join is wanted

Cardboard is a thick card that is used for constructing many of the pieces of furniture

Card is thinner and is used for backings and many of the smaller accessories

How to make an ORNAMENTAL FERN

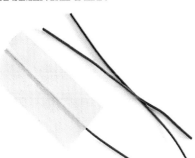

1 ~ Cut a length of green garden wire and cover two-thirds of both sides with a 1 in (2.5 cm) wide masking-tape strip.

2 ~ With sharp scissors or a scalpel, cut leaf shapes, removing some tape from in-between each leaf.

3 ~ Paint leaves with green acrylic paint. Group together at least six leaves and "plant" in a wad of self-hardening clay in a terracotta pot made of self-hardening clay. Water with care. Plants prefer a sunny exposure, and look effective in bathrooms and living rooms.

How to make a HAT BOX

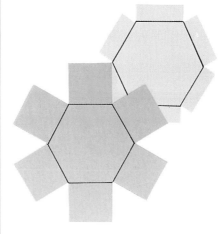

1 ~ From cardboard cut out appropriately-sized circles for the box and its lid, and mark the central hexagons. Cut away "v" shapes as shown.

2 ~ Using a straight edge and scissors, score along the hexagon lines. Very carefully, with your fingers, bend the sides into the middle.

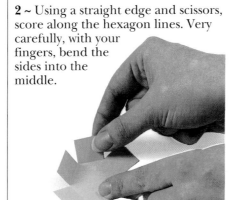

3 ~ Use pieces of masking tape to reinforce the corners of the box and its lid.

4 ~ Cover box with gift-wrap paper using a glue stick.

5 ~ Complete decoration with ribbon and flower trim as desired.

Useful Paper Items

A large variety of readily available paper products serve a multitude of functions in the dollhouse.

Stamps and illustrations from magazines and catalogs are ideal for pictures, children's games, scrap books, collections, and fire screens

Transfers, metallic strips, and gold stars can be used to provide ornamental detail on furniture and furnishings

Candy wrappers, particularly cellophane ones, can be used as decoration for boxes and jars and for gift wrapping

WORKING WITH
CLAY/MODELING MEDIUM

There are two major types of modeling material used in this book. One is a plastic medium, most often sold as Fimo, which needs to be baked to harden. The other preferred type is a self-hardening clay sold as Das.

Modeling medium comes in many colors and several textures so further painting is not normally required and it is good for recreating specialist "china" effects. Use a felt-tip pen to roll it out; the medium won't adhere to its nonstick surface. To make it malleable for use, warm it in your hands.

Because of its many colors it is ideal for creating food – everything from soup to nuts.

Self-hardening clay is more malleable to begin with but it only comes in neutral and terracotta. It can be softened with occasional sprays of water if it hardens prematurely. Before painting with an acrylic primer and acrylic or water-based paints, it needs to dry out for about 12 to 24 hours. This material is ideal for crockery that requires fine decoration or for anything with a handle.

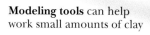

Modeling tools can help work small amounts of clay

Rolling pin is ideal for working large, flat amounts of modeling materials

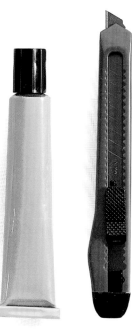

Glue should be strong, all-purpose clear adhesive (UHU)

Craft knife for cutting media

Modeling medium comes in a variety of shades

Water spray can be used for softening self-hardening clay

Waxed paper provides a nonstick surface when rolling out clay

Self-hardening clay comes in only two shades

How to make a PITCHER

1 ~ Roll clay to form a cylinder shape. Pinch and press cylinder to form a lip, flat top, waist, and bulbous base. Let dry.

2 ~ Sand to smooth away any rough edges.

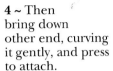

3 ~ Roll a long sausage shape for the handle. Spray pitcher to dampen and attach top end of handle, pressing gently.

4 ~ Then bring down other end, curving it gently, and press to attach.

5 ~ When pitcher is dry, sand gently. If handle falls off, it can be reattached by glue.

6 ~ Paint with primer and acrylic or water-based paints.

How to make a STRAWBERRY SHORTCAKE

1 ~ Roll out "pastry" and "cream" using tan and white modeling media; cut into strips. Make "berries".

2 ~ With pastry on bottom, cover with cream and strawberries. Repeat to form two layers.

3 ~ After baking, neaten edges with a sharp knife then cut into "slices" for serving.

How to make a CAULIFLOWER

1 ~ With white modeling medium make the "head". Use a pin to pick out the curds.

2 ~ Press balls of green modeling medium between finger and thumb. Curl the "leaves" in at the edges.

3 ~ Press the leaves against the head, overlapping them at the back until the cauliflower is complete.

How to make a PLATE

1 ~ Roll out clay on greaseproof paper so it is 1/8 in (3 mm) thick. With knife, roughly cut out shape – a square approximately 1 1/2 in (38 mm).

2 ~ With large pen top or other suitable cylinder, press into middle of square; the edges will lift. Raise the plate edges more, if necessary.

3 ~ Let plate dry and neaten edges with sandpaper before painting.

Sandpaper

Essential for producing a fine finish, particularly on large items such as the bathroom suite (see page 44), sandpaper comes in a number of grades. Start with coarse grade then apply finer sheets.

Color is not an indication of grain

Emery boards or small pieces of sandpaper wrapped around a pencil or small block of wood create ideal tools for refining small areas on modeled items

WORKING WITH
*W*OOD

When choosing wood, the most important thing is that it be free of knots and cracks. Sheets of $^1/_{16}$ in (2 mm) basswood (obeche) strip and single-ply plywood are the recommended craft woods. They are lightweight, easy to cut, and take well to staining. Spruce and pine are harder to work with. A great many other wood products come in handy for dollhouse decorating including dowel, squared strip, decorative moldings, and cocktail sticks. Always sand wood pieces before assembling so you have a nice, smooth finish, and stain before glueing (see right). Use fine sandpaper.

Masking tape is used to rough assemble pieces

Glue should be all-purpose, strong, clear plastic adhesive (UHU)

Rulers are necessary to mark measurements. A metal ruler can be used to cut against for a straight edge; a plastic ruler can be used to mark directly onto wood

Cutting tools include a craft knife

Basswood (obeche) comes in various thicknesses and widths; the widest is 3 in (75 mm). I've used $^1/_{16}$ in (2 mm) thick strip as my basic construction wood throughout the book

Squared strip comes in various widths and is used for legs, rails, and toy construction

Essential Woodworking Tools

A mini craft saw and miter box make dollhouse carpentry a snap. A miter box is essential for cutting squared corners and for getting a clean straight edge. It has indentations that match the standard craft wood widths so that your wood is held firmly. A lip at the front can be positioned at the edge of the workbench in case you need to apply traction.

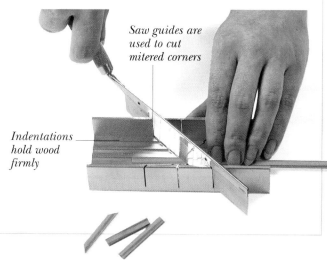

Saw guides are used to cut mitered corners

Indentations hold wood firmly

Single-ply plywood is thinner than basswood (obeche) but comes in larger widths. It is useful for the backs of wardrobes

Moldings

Sandpaper can be wound around a pencil and used to smooth curves

Cocktail sticks are useful for legs, umbrella handles, and plate racks

Basswood

Cocktail sticks

Dowel comes in various thicknesses and can be used for legs, rails, broom handles, and bedposts

Dowel

Squared strip

Single-ply plywood

Moldings can be used for decorative edgings

How to make a PICTURE FRAME

1 ~ Having selected your picture, decide on the size of the frame, i.e. whether it is to fit the picture exactly or accommodate a mount.

2 ~ Measure from outer edge to get accurate lengths then cut one back piece and four sides, mitering the corners of the sides.

3 ~ Stick picture to backing then glue on frame pieces. Attach to wall using a thread or wire handle or use double-sided tape.

How to make a KITCHEN SHELF

1 ~ Transfer templates to wood and cut out. Using a piece of sandpaper wrapped around a wooden block, sand pieces down to get a nice finish and to neaten curves.

2 ~ Check for fit by rough assembling pieces with masking tape. Stain with a proprietary product or strong tea, if desired (see below).

3 ~ When pieces are dry, apply glue to the sides and back and stick together. Then glue sides and back of shelves and slot into place. Hold unit with an rubber band until glue sets.

Staining

Pine or light oak is best achieved by strong tea

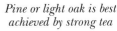

Water-based stains are available from most craft and DIY shops. Alway apply stain before glue as glue will form an impenetrable barrier and prevent the stain reaching the wood underneath. Brewed tea makes a good pine or light oak finish. Both tea and proprietary stain should be applied with a brush and several coats can be applied where a darker stain is wanted. Most stains are dry within 30 to 60 minutes. If you are adding a lace trim to resemble woodwork, this can be stained as well.

Dark oak or other hardwoods will require a proprietary wood stain

WORKING WITH
FABRICS

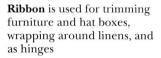

Fabrics are essential to the dollhouse decorator for pillows, cushions, curtains, wall hangings, tablecloths, bed linen and hangings, covering walls and floors, lining wardrobes and screens, and clothes. In addition to fabric, a wide range of trimmings and threads also comes in handy. An all-purpose, strong clear adhesive and a glue stick are useful for sticking fabric to furniture and dolls. Fabric sealer is a proprietary product sold to stop fraying; clear nail polish can be used.

Ribbon roses are good for finishing off bolsters, pillows, and hat boxes

Ribbon is used for trimming furniture and hat boxes, wrapping around linens, and as hinges

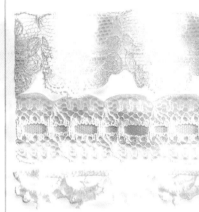

Lace fabric is used for doilies, tablecloths, curtains and trimmings; lace trim can be used as "carving" if stiffened by painting or staining

Fringe is used around the edge of furniture and for pelmets and canopies

Embroidery threads are used for dolls' hair, brush bristles, and for embroidered trim

Batting is essential for padding furniture and dolls; stuff it with lavender for a nice aroma

Toweling is used for bath mats, toilet covers, and towels. A stretchy terrycloth is ideal

Canvas and woven fabric is used for working carpets and rugs, stool covers, samplers, and cushions

Plush material can come in handy as carpeting or rugs, or on a large sofa. Satin is ideal for bed coverings and cushions

Small-scale patterns
Stripes, dots, and flowers on fabrics of different textures are the most suitable for decorating dollhouses.

Striped fabrics are a good choice for wall coverings, bed and table linen, and bolsters

Small florals contribute to a country-house feel for walls, upholstery, and window treatments

Dotted fabrics are effective for clothes and curtains

How to make a ROUND CUSHION

1 ~ Cut a 3^1/$_2$ in (90 mm) circle of fabric and piece of batting about 1^1/$_2$ in (38 mm) in diameter. Catch end with a running stitch and draw up to tighten.

2 ~ Finish off thread and cover opening with a ribbon rose or other trim.

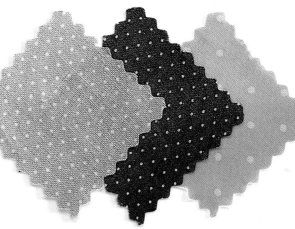

How to make a BOLSTER

1 ~ Cut a rectangular piece of fabric about 1^3/$_4$ in (44 mm) wide and 3 in (76 mm) long. Fold in half, right sides facing and sew down long side. Turn right side out.

2 ~ Roll a 1^1/$_2$ x 1 in (38 x 25 mm) piece of batting into a cylinder. Insert it into the fabric sleeve.

3 ~ Catch ends with running stitch and draw up tight. Tuck in any excess fabric at ends.

4 ~ Add ribbon trim and roses to each end to finish off.

WORKING WITH
*P*AINT

A selection of acrylic paints and a primer is all that is needed for paper, self-hardening clay and wood, but water colors can be used as well. Acrylic primer can be used on all materials as a base on which to add surface decoration. Gold and silver paints are ideal for creating metallic finishes, and a variety of felt-tips and markers can be used for creating embroidery effects on paper and fabric.

Acrylic paints and a primer are used for crockery, creating raised effects on furniture, for making doll's faces, and for strengthening furniture made of cardboard and paper. The acrylic primer dries quickly and gives a good surface to items making them take the paint better

Gold and silver paints are used for kitchen utensils, for making pails, faucets and knobs and for adding certain trims, such as on decorative boxes

Varnish should be used on self-hardening clay and wood to give a sheen and richness of effect. This should be an acetone-based clear varnish

Water colors such as a child's paintbox set come in handy for painting paper items or pictures

Felt-tip pens and markers add color to shower curtains and hot water bottle jackets, and are used for patchwork effects and lettering on sacks

WORKING WITH
Bits and Pieces

A variety of natural and manufactured items are ideal for using in a dollhouse. A walnut shell, for example, makes a fine baby's bed and small-scale foods can be substituted for the real thing. With a little imagination, you'll soon see an alternative use for practically every little object that you come across.

Beads of all types are useful. Little colored beads are ideal for knobs, pulls, and jewels while larger wooden beads are used as furniture feet. Crystal beads can be used as inkwells, and topped with smaller beads. Venetian or decorative beads can be used as vases or containers. Hollow beads can be used as goblets or dishes

Sequins can be used when creating bouquets and other flower arrangements

Pearls come in different sizes. Small ones can be dotted onto furniture and bedcovers, or used as jewelry, or drawer knobs

Felt-tip pen tops can be cut to size to form blender jars and milkshake glasses in stands of modeling medium

Buttons can be used as picture frames and as clock faces

Plastic containers can be shaped to use as inset glass doors on washing machines and dryers, or as cheese domes

Jewelry findings, which include small rings, nose studs, chains, and oval holders can be used for jewelry, picture frames, and hanging chains

Paper clips can be used as pendulums or trolley feet

Picture wire is useful for pail handles and for hanging pictures

Sponges both real and manufactured can be used as their full-grown cousins

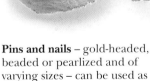

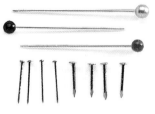

Pins and nails – gold-headed, beaded or pearlized and of varying sizes – can be used as drawer and door knobs

Dried beans and seeds can be painted and used for knobs; other "real" food can be used to stock kitchen canisters

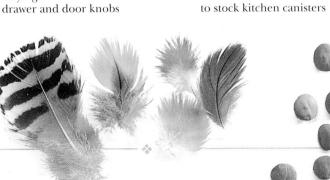

Feathers can be used in dusters and on dolls' hats

THE VICTORIAN
KITCHEN

This fully equipped downstairs kitchen is the scene of ceaseless activity. Cook is always in evidence, and the housemaids bustle in and out with tea trays and cleaning supplies. Furnishings are utilitarian with few creature comforts for the staff. The old cast-iron stove, with its ever-burning fire, requires constant feeding, and the range of cast-iron pots hints at the number of hungry mouths to feed.

The big dresser to the left houses a variety of staple items in its cupboards while the shelves hold several storage canisters. Nearby, jams and preserves are stored on a wall-hung unit.

Next to the range, a small wooden table, useful for holding cooking utensils, sits beneath a drying rack. The large butler's sink to the right is supported on pillars of "brick" and has a "Delft tile" splashback to match that of the range. Only cold water comes out of the faucet; hot water is heated in the kettle.

The large central pine table is where most of the food is prepared. It has to be big enough for rolling out pastry and sorting the produce from the kitchen garden or greengrocer's. When it is below stairs' tea time, the table is set with crockery and the high-backed chairs are drawn up close.

The big Welsh dresser by the window is where the china is kept. When not in use, the cutlery is stored in its commodious drawers.

Organically grown produce
Untouched by harmful fertilizers and sprays, the weekly produce delivery, made from modeling medium, has to be sorted and stored.

Drying rack for dishes
has cocktail stick slotted
shelves that fit into wood strip
back and sides

Welsh dresser
has embroidered ribbon
trim added to its top for a
sprightly decorative finish

Housemaid's box
of wood strip
has black model-
ing medium
"wrought iron"
handle and
brackets

Towel rack
is made from
squared strip
pieces taped
together

Floor rug
has fringe made by
removing several woof threads
from its woven fabric

Wallcovering and floor
– the one being a flower-sprigged
fabric, the other brick paper sheeting
– approximate to Victorian originals

THE VICTORIAN
Kitchen Catalog

Dinner service
All manner of gaily colored plates, platters, cups, saucers, tureens, bowls, sauceboats, and other eating and serving crockery can be created from self-hardening clay shaped and then painted. See page 11 for how-to instructions.

Farm-fresh vegetables
Not a trace of pests or weather damage on a range of produce modeled to please. No doll-house child would dare leave over his or her vegetables. See page 11 for tips.

The kitchen clock
A coin-sized circle of modeling medium has a smaller white face painted on it; numbers and hands are picked out in black.

Baskets, bags, and boxes
The essential containers for a range of stock ingredients are created out of paper, fabric, and modeling medium. The potatoes, mushrooms, apples, and eggs are of modeling medium, too.

Delicious edibles
The groaning board will be limited only by your imagination and skill in modeling foodstuffs for every meal; see page 28 for more.

Calendar
Frozen in time or kept up to date, an old-fashioned farmhouse calendar of plywood and paper is easy to read.

Spice storage
Tiny pieces of wood are all that's needed to make the drawers to house your spice selection and a box to keep salt running free.

Jugs and bowls
Pitchers for pouring cream, milk, and juice, and bowls to house fresh-picked strawberries, ice creams, and puddings are shaped out of self-hardening clay and painted in delicate patterns. See page 11 for how-to instructions.

Cutlery and metal containers
A coat of metallic paint can conceal the duller finish of modeling medium and result in impressive looking silver tableware, and chrome or copper cookware. The pail is made from paper painted silver, and then given a fuse-wire handle; see page 66.

Pots and pans
Sturdy cookware designed to withstand the heat of the old-fashioned range can be made in a variety of styles from modeling medium; the heat-driven irons are similarly created.

Home-made preserves
Rows of gingham-covered jars housing last summer's bounty can stock larder shelves or be put out on display. Make them out of modeling medium in the appropriate colors to reflect the contents.

Floor-cleaning materials
Mops, brooms, brushes, dustpans, and other assorted sweeping gear can be fashioned out of dowel or cocktail sticks and given embroidery thread or modeling medium bristles.

Baking utensils
A rolling pin and an assortment of mixing spoons are modeled to look like wood. The mortar and pestle are well served by the original substance.

Cleaning box
The wood strip and modeling medium box contains brushes, with embroidery thread bristles, shoe polish of modeling medium, a fabric cleaning rag, and a real feather duster.

THE VICTORIAN
$\mathcal{K}$ITCHEN $\mathcal{F}$URNITURE

"Pine" finish comes from staining with tea

KITCHEN DRESSER

Ideal for displaying crockery or holding ample supplies, two dressers can be created from the templates on page 68. The Welsh dresser shown here and described on page 69 uses all the templates except for the base and drawer panel. For an open-shelved one, use the drawer panel front, add an extra shelf, and finish with the base piece.

LARGE RECTANGULAR TABLE

Similar in construction to the small rectangular table, see right, this has a 3 x 5 in (75 x 125 mm) wood strip top.

Four $^1/_2$ in (12 mm) wide side pieces of wood strip – two of 2 $^9/_{16}$ in (65 mm), and two of 4 $^9/_{16}$ in (115 mm) – should be glued together to make the support frame for the top.

Four legs 2 $^9/_{16}$ in (65 mm) long should be cut from squared strip and glued one into each corner. Two 2 $^1/_8$ in

(55 mm) squared strip pieces are used for cross braces to hold shelf.

A 1 $^9/_{16}$ x 4 $^5/_{16}$ in (40 x 110 mm) piece of single-ply plywood forms a lower shelf and is glued to the cross braces.

Two wood drawer fronts, 1 $^1/_4$ x $^1/_4$ in (32 x 6 mm), have modeling medium knobs glued on.

To finish off the curves, wrap a piece of sandpaper around a pencil and use to sand away any excess wood

Decorative ribbon trim is glued to a thin strip of wood then attached to the dresser

Legs are of $^1/_4$ in (6 mm) squared strip

Top and frame are made of wood strip

Paper "tile" easy-to-clean surface

SINK UNIT

This sturdy butler's sink of self-hardening clay painted with white acrylic stands on two massive wooden supports – $1^3/_4$ deep x $^5/_8$ wide x 2 in high (45 mm x 16 mm x 52 mm) – covered in brick paper.

The splashback is a piece of cardboard, 3 x $4^1/_2$ in (75 x 115 mm), painted white. It is decorated with tile-printed paper, and supports a tap of gray modeling medium.

Integral shelf to store pots and pans

KITCHEN STOVE

Essential for hot water and heat, this solid fuel-burning range of cardboard painted with black acrylic, has its templates on pages 78-79.

Hinges cut from gold stars

Fire of red, orange, yellow, and black tissue paper

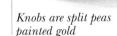

SMALL RECTANGULAR TABLE

One or more of these "pine" tables with integral drawer are very handy in a kitchen for storing utensils or holding plates of food. Full making-up instructions and templates are on page 69.

Knobs are split peas painted gold

HIGH-BACKED CHAIR

Any number of these simple "pine" kitchen chairs can be created using the templates and written instructions for the wooden chair on page 80. They also look nice with decorative seat cushions (see page 28).

THE MODERN
*K*ITCHEN

Today's kitchens are compact and efficient places. Because they often have to perform more than one function, they may contain a wide range of electrically powered appliances. Food preparation, of course, remains the vital consideration when planning a kitchen: as well as feeding their families a healthy diet, modern cooks are concerned that food preparation be quick and easy, so today's kitchens come equipped with many labor-saving devices.

*F*resh fruit
Watermelon slices, grapes, and bananas of modeling medium are a colorful and healthful addition in any kitchen. They make an ideal snack or a delicious dessert.

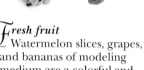

*V*egetable medley
Today's generation enjoys peppers, broccoli, tomatoes, cabbage, mushrooms, asparagus, and cucumbers in salads, and new potatoes simply boiled. The vegetables are freshly modeled. The mushroom box is paper, the basket modeling medium, and the potato dirt, cocoa.

*C*ake tins
Gaily decorated paper containers hold tea-time snacks of cookies and an iced chocolate cake. The cookies and cake, including the glacé cherries, are all created from modeling medium.

*E*lectrical appliances
The tea kettle and blender base are modeled while the microwave is cardboard.

*E*veryday dishes
An assortment of plates and mugs are created from self-hardening clay and are decorated with a sprightly flower motif. They are dishwasher safe.

*K*itchen knives
Silver painted paper blades are set into modeling medium handles. They are stored on a silver paper-and-wood rack.

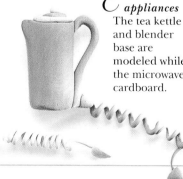

*B*ulletin board and holder
Ideal for displaying shopping lists and reminders, the board is constructed of paper and wood. Paper towels are stored on a wall-mounted holder.

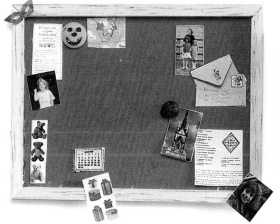

*S*pice rack
A variety of dried herbs and spices are stored in jars of modeling medium set on a wall-hung wooden unit. The two storage drawers have gold headed pin pulls.

*G*lass canisters
The jars are made from plastic tubes, used to hold glitter, and the tops are of modeling medium. They store millet "puffed rice", whole-wheat spaghetti, flour, and sesame seed "dried beans".

*I*ron and board
The wooden board with fabric and silver tape trim stands on painted wire legs. The steam iron is made of modeling medium.

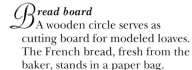

*B*read board
A wooden circle serves as cutting board for modeled loaves. The French bread, fresh from the baker, stands in a paper bag.

The Efficiency Kitchen

Where space is at a premium, furnishings need to maximize the available space. A stacking cardboard washer and dryer have plastic-lid windows set in a silver painted and tape trim surround. These halve the amount of floor space normally required. The wooden stool and paper-and-wire storage unit can be stored under the wood, bead, and dowel worktop.

THE COLONIAL
*K*ITCHEN

Popular with period decorators, American colonial interiors have a particular rustic charm. Lacking any modern comforts and conveniences, inhabitants of dollhouses of the time will have to make do with mainly plain and unadorned kitchen equipment and accessories. In addition to their often rough and ready designs, they are notable for their being constructed of widely available materials – wood, straw, and clay.

*S*torage boxes
These Shaker oval shapes, decorative and functional, are made from painted paper with wooden bases and lids.

*C*andles and holders
"Tin" sconces, pierced for decoration and hanging, are made of silver painted paper. Thin wooden rectangles are joined to make a box for the candles; the latter are made of modeling medium.

*C*ooking utensils
The slotted spoon and knife blades are made from thick silver foil; the handle is modeling medium. The wooden spoons are modeled.

*T*he kitchen garden produce
Peas, sweetcorn, cabbage, cauliflower, pumpkins, and radishes form a large part of the daily fare. All, including the braided basket and clay bowl, are created from modeling medium except for the ears of corn, which are buttons.

*F*irewood and axes
A modeled log basket holds a pile of wood. Perhaps these "logs" were hewn from hawthorn twigs using the tree and hand axes constructed of modeling medium.

*P*ie safe
Placed high up on the wall, out of the reach of rodents and little hands, this wooden storage unit with its pierced "tin" panels of paper painted silver, is where freshly baked goods are stored. In certain cases, it may be fitted with a lock.

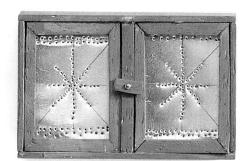

Pioneering Pastimes

The hub of colonial life is the kitchen and there, a dollhouse denizen will find lots to do. The fire needs feeding for the cooking pot or hot water, clothes need washing, produce from the garden needs sorting and preparing and, when there is a spare moment, there's always the mending to pick up and see to.

Clothes washing paraphernalia

The wash tub of painted paper and the clothes scrubber – painted paper with wooden sides – are familiar kitchen items as the open fire provided the hot water needed for cleaning clothes. The modeled clothes pins in their felt holder would have hung on a nearby wall until needed.

Hat rack

Brass headed pins on two rectangular wooden strips make a simple and effective storage place. The pouches, used for holding powder and bullets, were made of leather scraps, while the gardening hat was created from braided straw and has a beaded trim.

Patchwork

Miniature fabric squares are glued to a backing to suggest the floor coverings created from worn-out clothes. The sewing threads and pin cushion are of modeling medium, the box is wood.

Canisters and jugs

The "stoneware" canisters, made of modeling medium, are useful for keeping dry goods, such as sugar and flour, free from pests while the jugs store cider, maple syrup, and molasses.

FOOD FROM THE KITCHEN

Any dollhouse cook worth her salt must be able to provide three square meals a day, and a host of party and special occasion dishes. Luckily, all he or she needs is modeling material in a variety of colors, some self-hardening clay or buttons for the plates, and proper photographic reference. Then every culinary occasion – from Sunday brunch through to a tea party, picnic, or even Christmas dinner – can be celebrated in style.

Glorious Cakes
Chocolate cupcakes, each topped with a cherry or candy, accompany a lemon layer cake covered with marzipan icing. These, plus the Black Forest gâteau, are sure to suit every doll's sweet tooth. The plates are made similar to those on page 11, and painted white with a gold trim.

Perfect Pastries
Chocolate cream pie in a chocolate pastry crust, slices of jelly roll, and cream filled chocolate and pastry rolls, are ideal tea-time treats. For the jelly roll effect, top a rectangular layer of brown "cake" with one of white and roll up both together.

Middle Eastern Specialties
Pita breads filled with salad and meat or cheese are on offer alongside lamb kebabs threaded onto pins.

All-American Fare
Hamburgers in buns with fries and a salad garnish are standard snack-time orders. Serve with plenty of modeled tomato ketchup and salt and pepper.

A Christmas Feast
The traditional golden roasted turkey, mince pies, and plum pudding are joined by a selection of fresh vegetables including carrots, peas, and potatoes, with a fresh berry cocktail to follow.

The Festive Table
Dressed in a seasonal cloth with bows and golden trim, the best bead goblets and "china" plates are complemented by the wreathed candle centerpiece. Paper crackers are there for the pulling.

Meals For All Occasions
Party planning was never easier for the dollhouse entertainer. Modeling medium is ideal for creating a vast number of special dishes suitable for all types of meals. Set food on a piece of the appropriate fabric, accompany with matching napkins or paper decorations, serve on a few painted self-hardening clay plates, and you can create the culinary ambiance of your choice.

Different colored party streamers add to the fun

"Plates" are white plastic buttons in dinner and serving plate sizes

A small amount of fabric is all that is required to make a cloth and napkin set

A **Child's Party**
Make it a really special occasion by serving up food certain to please the younger set – hot dogs, chunks of cheese, ice cream cones and sundaes, iced cookies, jello, and a rose decorated pink-frosted cake.

S **unday Brunch**
Platefuls of eggs, bacon, and sausage are salmonella- and cholesterol-free. Enjoy them with mushrooms and broiled tomatoes. Select toast or the breakfast roll of your choice and spread with butter or strawberry jam.

H **igh Tea**
This substantial early evening meal, first indulged in over a century ago, is made up primarily of cold meats, savory pies, and sandwiches. A more contemporary addition is the selection of imported cheeses.

Pies and terrines can be recreated with a variety of fillings and in all the traditional shapes

Red-topped Edam and ripe Brie accompany two foil-wrapped cheeses

THE VICTORIAN
*M*ASTER
*B*EDROOM

*W*ild flower print
of dried forget-me-nots
complements delicate floral
wallpaper

***Off limits to all but the littlest one, the master
bedroom's decoration owes much to Mama's taste.***
She regards it as her refuge from the cares of running a
large house. Although she has little time for breakfast in
bed now that baby has arrived, today is a special day.
Along with morning tea in her special china set, a
beautiful bouquet, to mark her wedding anniversary,
arrived on the breakfast tray.

Pride of place in the room is held by the grand four-
poster, one item of the bedroom suite that formed part
of her dowry. The moiré satin bed hangings,
bolster, and coverlet were imported from
France, created to her specifications. The
fabric-covered dressing table with lace trim and
the pearl-buttoned boudoir chair complete the set.
Set on top of the dressing table is Mama's
jewelry casket, grooming set, and some jars
of face cream. Displayed on the small table
next to the bed and on the walls are a
number of family photographs.

Mama also brought some other
good furniture pieces with her on her
marriage. These include the antique
sewing basket, of which she makes much
use – with the children and
household furnishings to see to –
and the mahogany chest of drawers.

Papa's silk vest, only worn
on special days, is displayed on the
wooden valet; he will wear it today
to please Mama.

*L*ace-skirted cradle
of eggshells with fabric
trim makes a snug bed for
baby

Four-poster bed of cardboard and wooden dowel has elaborate moiré satin bed hangings

Family photographs are miniature illustrations set in jewelry finding frames

Anniversary bouquet *contains beads set on sequins held by embroidery thread*

Modesty screen of wooden panels has transfer decoration

Parasols are fabric scraps glued to cocktail sticks and topped with beads

Mama's little luxuries
A present of a Paris hat, in its beautiful beribboned box, and lace parasol brings a twinkle to her eyes.

THE VICTORIAN
MASTER BEDROOM CATALOG

Dressing table accessories
Modeling medium is used for the lavender wand drawer fresheners, brushes, and pin cushion base.

Table-top mirror
Silvered plastic "mirror" is glued to a wooden frame. Two drawers with bead pulls store delicate fabric hankies. The stud boxes are buttons.

Tea service
Delicate milk glass tea set with matching cups and saucers is arranged on cloth-covered wooden tray. The china and lemon cake slices are all of modeling medium.

Hat boxes
Floral patterned fabric is glued to circular cardboard boxes decorated with ribbon and lace trim and used for protecting special-occasion hats. Placed on top of a wardrobe they are pretty and practical storage items. See page 9 for how-to.

Hats and bonnets
Scraps of satin, wool, and felt fabrics are augmented by feathers and ribbon trims to produce a range of headwear suitable for most occasions.

Family jewels
A casket (and key) of silver wedding-cake trim stores jewelry constructed of wire, beads, and brilliants.

Parasols
Lengths of satin fabric with ribbon and lace trim are furled around painted cocktail sticks with bead ends.

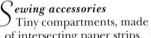

Flower prints
The tiniest forget-me-nots are dried, mounted on paper, and then attached to a wooden frame. The frames are then "hung" on the wall by means of double-sided tape.

Flower bouquet
Delicate beaded and sequinned "flowers" on French knot embroidered foliage are glued to tissue paper surround and held by a ribbon trim.

Frames
Portraits of family members, cut from stamps, are held in gold wire jewelry findings. Some can be wall hung; others, with cardboard backings, can be set out on a surface protected by a doily of lacy fabric.

Sewing accessories
Tiny compartments, made of intersecting paper strips, hold a range of modeled sewing threads in various different shades. They fit into the top of the sewing box so that essential supplies are always at working height. The scissors are cut from the heavy foil wrapping on wine bottles, and the spare buttons are culled from the bead box. A supply of real lace and ribbon also is useful to have on hand.

Fashionable footwear
A range of suitable walking and evening shoes are created from modeling medium to match the owner's day-time and formal dresses. When not being worn, these are stored in fabric-covered paper shoe boxes with ribbon trim.

Gentleman's accessories
The dumb valet, made of thin rectangular wooden pieces attached to a hanger-shaped top, holds a brightly patterned silk vest. A hidden central shelf contains cufflinks and dress-shirt studs. A pair of sturdy laced shoes, made of modeling medium, can be stored under the bed in their fabric-covered paper box when not needed.

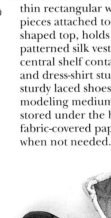

Display shelf
This triangular wooden shelving unit is ideal for siting in a corner. It holds a crystal bead vase with a sprig of dried flowers and an amythyst crystal – one of the many geological specimens Papa collects.

THE VICTORIAN
Master Bedroom Furniture

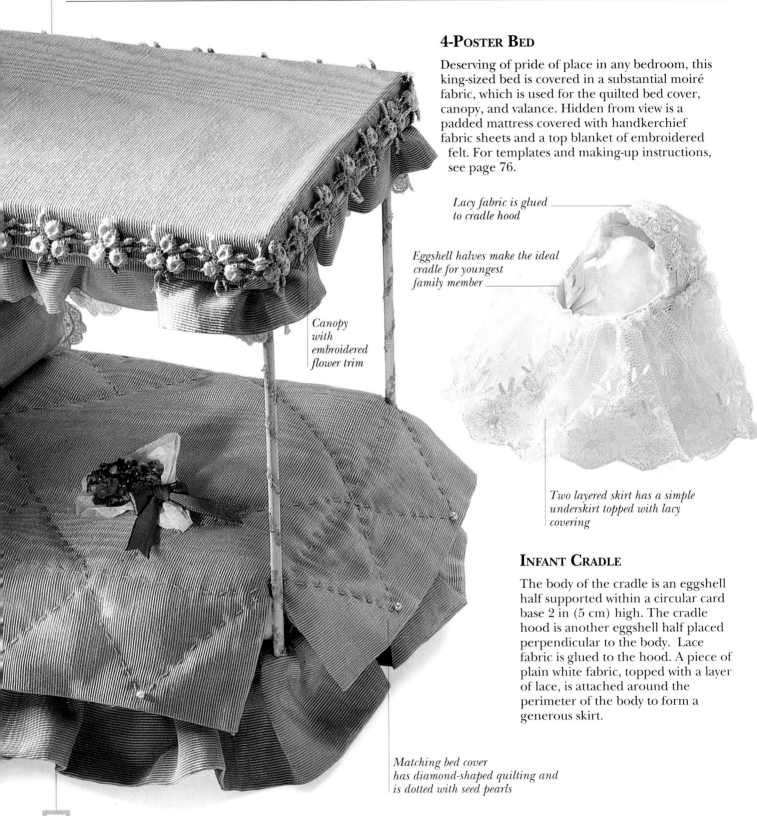

4-POSTER BED

Deserving of pride of place in any bedroom, this king-sized bed is covered in a substantial moiré fabric, which is used for the quilted bed cover, canopy, and valance. Hidden from view is a padded mattress covered with handkerchief fabric sheets and a top blanket of embroidered felt. For templates and making-up instructions, see page 76.

Lacy fabric is glued to cradle hood

Eggshell halves make the ideal cradle for youngest family member

Canopy with embroidered flower trim

Two layered skirt has a simple underskirt topped with lacy covering

INFANT CRADLE

The body of the cradle is an eggshell half supported within a circular card base 2 in (5 cm) high. The cradle hood is another eggshell half placed perpendicular to the body. Lace fabric is glued to the hood. A piece of plain white fabric, topped with a layer of lace, is attached around the perimeter of the body to form a generous skirt.

Matching bed cover has diamond-shaped quilting and is dotted with seed pearls

Mahogany finish is produced by wood stain

Transfer motif is rubbed on or glued to each frame

MODESTY SCREEN

Made of wood strip pieces stained a darker shade and joined with masking tape, see page 69 for templates and instructions, this has a "gold leaf" rub-down decorative trim.

Wedding cake trim is used to decorate casket

CHEST OF DRAWERS

The pearl-knobbed deep drawers of this wooden chest hold substantial amounts of garments. Full making-up instructions and templates are on page 75.

DRESSING TABLE

Along with its matching chair, this is part of a furniture suite that includes the 4-poster bed. Full making-up instructions and templates are found on page 66.

BOUDOIR CHAIR

The base is a $1^1/_2$ in (4 cm) card cube and the back is made from two $3^1/_2$ x $1^9/_{16}$ in (9 x 4 cm) card rectangles with angled tops. First the cube base is covered in the moiré fabric. Then the front-facing back piece is covered with batting and topped with fabric, and the second fabric-covered piece is glued to it, back to back. This gives a neat effect.

The back is then glued to one side of the cube. For the seat's trim apply cut-out lace and decorative ribbon.

Attach seed pearls to the chair back. Make a cushion from matching fabric, and fill with sand to weight it.

Cushion is filled with sand to plump it up

Carved trim is lace that is stained and glued in place

SEWING BOX

The separate compartments are ideal for holding a collection of sewing implements, trimmings, and threads at table-top height. For templates and making-up instructions, see page 67.

THE VICTORIAN

Girl's Bedroom

Hatboxes, trimmed in ribbon and lace, are easy to construct from card; see instructions page 9

A girl's bedroom affords wonderful opportunities for making furnishings and accessories with a truly feminine feel. What young lady, no matter the era, could resist a dreamy half-tester bed dressed with pristine linen and a matching coverlet, or a wardrobe filled with cotton shifts and frilly dresses.

The pink-painted furniture harkens back to an earlier time but is just as pleasing to the contemporary child; this is a room where childhood dreams are encouraged and inspired. A bedside table can be used to hold ornaments or take a period pitcher and bowl, while the linen-topped fabric covered table is an attractive surface when she wants to draw or write. The tiny ribbon-trimmed stool and flouncy fabric chair are ideal for sitting or for putting things on.

The room is filled with items to keep a small one amused and there is a plethora of pretty, ribbon bedecked hatboxes to store toys and accessories.

A combination of floral patterns on the furniture and walls gives an English country-house feel to the room. Delightful touches such as the rose tie-backs on the curtains and embroidered flowers on the linens help to accentuate the floral theme. The commercially made wall lights are attuned to the period; everything else is hand-made, from the simply stitched sampler to the needlepointed rug.

Half-tester bed, with its matching valance and quilted coverlet, has embroidered linens of fine cotton. Making-up instructions are on page 41

Embroidered sampler, created from fine woven fabric and silk thread, is held in a mitered frame

Accessories *are fashioned from fabric and modeling medium.*

Dollhouse comes with all fixtures and furnishings. Templates and instructions are on page 73

Dolly has painted bead face and modeling medium body. Her hair is embroidery thread

Toybox treasures
The teddy of self-hardening clay is a favorite toy as are the jump rope (seen above) made from crochet thread and beads, the pull-along lamb, and scrap book.

Floor carpet is a piece of heavy duty plush fabric cut to size

THE VICTORIAN
Girl's Room Catalog

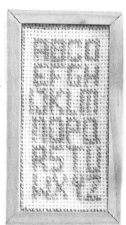

Sampler
A small rectangle of woven fabric is covered in letters picked out in fine silk diagonal threads. It is set within a mitered frame; for framing hints, see page 13.

Nursery animals
No self-respecting dollhouse child would be without one or two of these painted clay bears. The lamb pull-toy is created from black pipe cleaners covered with bits of fleece.

A trio of dollies
Bead heads, covered in embroidery thread and set on wire bodies padded with masking tape, are covered by scraps of fabric glued to fit.

Slippers, shoes, and hangers
Embroidered terry toweling scuffs sit next to modeling medium shoes with bead trim. The wire hangers are covered in fabric scraps.

Hats
Bits of felt and ribbon are finished off with rose ribbons.

Scraps
Decorative scraps and illustrations cut from magazines can be stored in a ribbon-topped box until there is time to stick them down in paper books.

Ornamental mirror
Foil stuck to a plastic backing has a card support. Blobs of acrylic paint form the raised decorative edge.

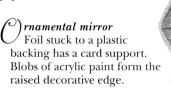

Traveling hat boxes
These fabric-covered card containers with lace and ribbon trim come complete with embroidery thread handles for carrying. Tips on their construction can be found on page 9.

A Modern Teenager

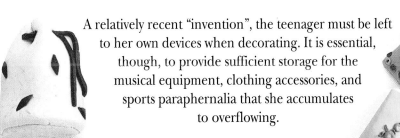

A relatively recent "invention", the teenager must be left to her own devices when decorating. It is essential, though, to provide sufficient storage for the musical equipment, clothing accessories, and sports paraphernalia that she accumulates to overflowing.

Art materials Paint set and crayon pencils in decorated cases are all made from modeling medium.

Hot wheels White leather red-wheeled roller skates with matching satchel for accessories are made from modeling medium.

Telephone Modeling medium phone with painted dial has plastic spiral cord.

Musical gear A selection of cassette players is essential unless one wants to get out of step with the music. All are modeled.

Sweet Sixteen

Today's teenager, when home, is rarely found without her earphones or telephone! Her life is one social whirl and with all the necessary gear in tow, she is free to try her hand at a whole range of activities.

Shoulderbag Roomy enough to hold all a girl's make-up and money, this modeled "leather" handbag has "brass" jewelry finding clasp and buckles.

Outdoor accessories Modeling medium is ideal for creating waterproof accessories such as the pairs of rubber sandals, the drawstring beach bag, the high-factor sun lotions, and the polarized sun glasses.

THE VICTORIAN
Girl's Room Furniture

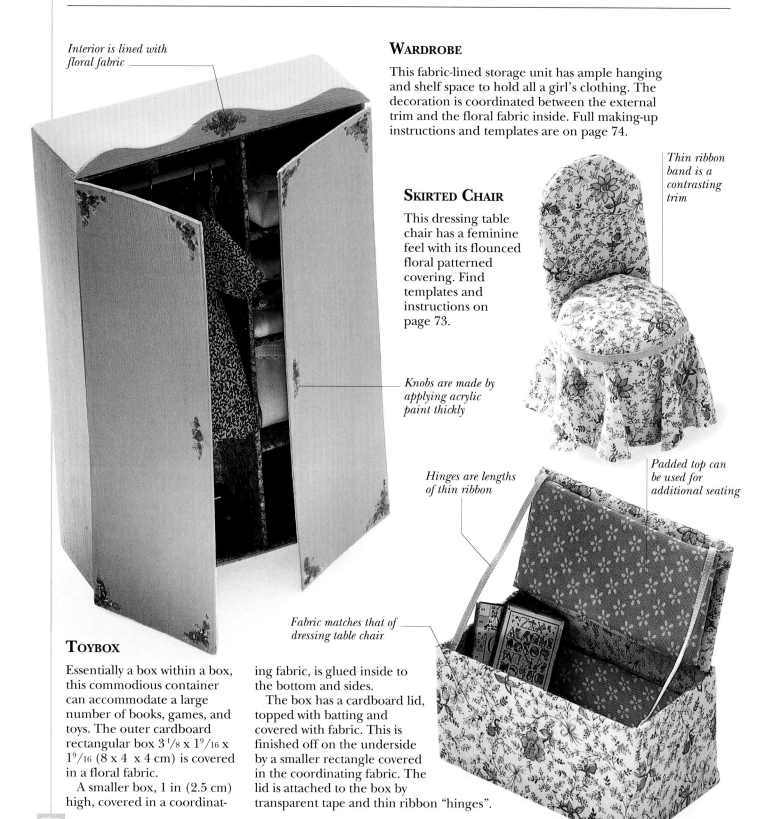

Interior is lined with floral fabric

WARDROBE

This fabric-lined storage unit has ample hanging and shelf space to hold all a girl's clothing. The decoration is coordinated between the external trim and the floral fabric inside. Full making-up instructions and templates are on page 74.

SKIRTED CHAIR

This dressing table chair has a feminine feel with its flounced floral patterned covering. Find templates and instructions on page 73.

Thin ribbon band is a contrasting trim

Knobs are made by applying acrylic paint thickly

Hinges are lengths of thin ribbon

Padded top can be used for additional seating

Fabric matches that of dressing table chair

TOYBOX

Essentially a box within a box, this commodious container can accommodate a large number of books, games, and toys. The outer cardboard rectangular box $3\frac{1}{8}$ x $1\frac{9}{16}$ x $1\frac{9}{16}$ (8 x 4 x 4 cm) is covered in a floral fabric.

A smaller box, 1 in (2.5 cm) high, covered in a coordinat-ing fabric, is glued inside to the bottom and sides.

The box has a cardboard lid, topped with batting and covered with fabric. This is finished off on the underside by a smaller rectangle covered in the coordinating fabric. The lid is attached to the box by transparent tape and thin ribbon "hinges".

WASHSTAND

Pink-painted wash-stand has decorative curved detailing on its back and front. Useful for storing a girl's bits and pieces, instructions and templates are on page 72.

Pillows are embroidered with floral motif

Single-sized bed is made of cardboard and has fabric bedding

HALF-TESTER BED

A close relative of the 4-poster found in the master bedroom, this dreamy girl's bed can be made by adapting the templates and instructions found on pages 76-78. A cardboard base should be formed that is 3 in (78 mm) wide. A valance is created similarly to its larger relative, then neatened by a fabric-covered top piece.

The headboard of $3\,^5/_{16}$ x $6\,^1/_8$ in (85 x 155 mm) cardboard is attached to the back; two fabric-covered sides, $1\,^3/_4$ x $6\,^1/_8$ in (45 x 155 mm), and a fabric-covered top, $3\,^5/_{16}$ x $1\,^{11}/_{16}$ in (85 x 43 mm), are joined to it.

The half-tester top is a slightly larger rectangle, approximately $3\,^1/_8$ x $1\,^3/_4$ x $^1/_2$ in (90 x 45 x 12 mm). This is covered in fabric and has a ruffle, trimmed with lace, glued to its under side. Two lace-trimmed curtains also are added before the tester is glued firmly to the top of the headboard. Ribbon rose tie-backs and a quilted coverlet complete the bed clothes. The pillowcases are embroidered with rose buds.

Lace-trimmed curtains are glued to back

Open-weave fabric can be embroidered

CIRCULAR TABLE

Identical to the sitting room table but covered in a calico skirt with woven top, the instructions and templates are on page 72.

A Victorian Boy

Less sophisticated than his modern-day counterpart, the 19th century boy is surrounded by a selection of leather-bound books, sports equipment, and sturdy toys and playthings that provide his amusement. He depends on his teddy bear for comfort.

Paper kites
Made like their bigger brothers from wood strips and paper but with thread twine, these can sail across a boy's room as well as the sky.

Drum and sticks
When he wants to sound off, our boy uses paper drum with plastic sticks cut from a comb.

School books
Bound in modeling medium "leather", these are for reading, 'riting and 'rithmatic.

Bat, ball, and box
Wood was used for the bat and box; the ball and Jack were modeled.

Boat scenes
Wood scrap frames enclose two miniature sailboats made of red-painted wood, with painted paper sails and pennants.

Slatted bed
This single bed has a head- and footboard of wood strip and legs of ¼ in (6 mm) squared strip. The frame is squared strip with wood slats. All are stained. The bedding consists of a batting mattress covered with fine cotton sheets and woven fabric throw. The pipe-cleaner teddy is often found sleeping there.

Tug and sail boat
The small wooden tug for bathtub use is made from painted squared strip. The "ocean-going" yacht has a modeling medium hull with contrasting portholes and deck. The painted greaseproof paper sails are set on a cocktail stick mast. The boat flies a paper pennant.

A Modern Boy

As he lies on his duvet-covered Scandinavian-style bed, the modern boy can look around him and see the effect of science on his toys and lifestyle. Where his Victorian forebear relied mainly on muscle power and natural materials, today's youngster depends on silicon chips, electricity, batteries, and plastic. His spare time is spent on engaging in sporting events or playing computer games – at which he is a whiz.

Sports equipment
The "Louisville slugger" bat and baseball are of modeling medium as are the ice skates.

Telephone and computer
The slim-line telephone of modeling medium has plastic spiral cord. The PC's keyboard and monitor also are modeled.

Bulletin board and basket
Paper board in mitered wooden frame holds current memorabilia while the paper waste basket holds yesterday's.

Racing set
The cars have bead wheels and are directed by handsets to run on the "electrified" oval track. All are made from modeling medium.

Unpainted pine
When choosing furniture for a child, pick something that can be self-assembled and is easy to care for. This bed has plain wooden strip sides that can be glued around a cardboard base. The squared strip legs are added last. Foam mattress is topped with fitted sheets and duvet.

THE VICTORIAN
ℬATHROOM

Ornamental cistern
is a lace-trimmed rectangular
wooden box overpainted with
white acrylic

Although it is free of many plumbing restrictions, a doll's house bathroom still must provide scope for its occupants to perform all necessary functions. Today's families often have to make do with only very small bathrooms but Victorian bathrooms, where fitted, were commodious and fixtures were large scale.

A glass-fronted linen cupboard stores freshly starched sheets and fluffy towels; towels in use are kept near at hand on a wooden rail. Beauty and body care supplies are displayed on wall-hung shelves, and shaving supplies in the mirrored cabinet above the sink. The wooden washstand, with shell mirror overhead, houses a hot water bottle, decorative pitcher and basin, soap dish, and dusting powder.

A floral patterned fabric wallcovering is soothing to contemplate while soaking in the bath, and a selection of houseplants – African violets, spider plant, and fern – chosen for enjoying a humid atmosphere, add a touch of greenery displayed on their wooden plant stands.

A folding screen provides the necessary privacy where children about to be bathed can change. The pelmeted window drapes protect the bather from cool breezes while his or her feet are cushioned from the cold marble floor by the woven bath rug.

In case of emergencies, a plunger and pail are within easy reach of the toilet.

A good soak
Mama, at least her capped head and shoulders, lies in a dish washing liquid foam bath and is happy for her few minutes' peace and quiet.

Delicate fern is created from masking tape and garden wire. See page 9 for instructions

Porcelain and crystal jars are made from decorative beads. See page 17 for further inspiration

Wallcovering is a water-resistant floral patterned fabric

Decorative mirror is made from the tiniest sea shells stuck onto silvered glass

Grooming accessories are created from painted self-hardening clay and fabric

Sanitary suite of basin, bathtub, and toilet comes with stenciled decoration and "brass" faucets

THE VICTORIAN
*B*ATHROOM *C*ATALOG

*B*ath accessories
Glued wood strips, cotton wool, embroidery thread, and natural sponge can be used to make an assortment of useful items such as the draining platform, bath tray, washing sponges, and back and nail brushes.

*O*pen cupboard and toiletries
Made of stained and varnished wooden pieces, the cupboard consists of three shelves and two sides fixed to a curved back. A range of perfumes and body lotions, in jars of crystal beads, are arrayed on the shelves. The storage boxes are small blocks of wood covered with wrapping paper.

*S*pider plant and violets
Long leaves are masking tape on fine wire (see page 9) while the smaller leaves and pots are of self-hardening clay.

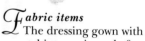

*T*oilet roll holder and hooks
These are made from pieces of varnished wood and one or more golden-headed pins. Thin metal wire is bent around the toilet paper, carefully cut from tissues and rolled up.

*F*abric items
The dressing gown with matching cap is made from cotton remnants. A floral pattern suits the toilet bag, while the mules and moccasins are of felt with masking tape soles. A swatch of striped fabric suited the bath mat. Fringe is created by pulling some threads from the sides.

*P*lunger and pail
A cocktail-stick handle and modeled cap make the plunger; templates for the pail are on page 66.

*D*usting powder set
The box is floral paper fixed to circular shapes; the puff is cotton wool.

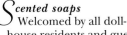

*S*cented soaps
Welcomed by all doll-house residents and guests, a selection of perfumed favorites are created from beads, or balls of modeling medium, covered with tissue paper and a decorative seal. Finely patterned floral papers are wrapped around rectangular wooden blocks and/or cardboard shapes for the boxes and lids.

*G*entleman's cupboard
Complete with foil mirror and beaded handle this shelved, varnished wooden unit contains all the shaving gear a man could crave. Shaving soap and badger brush of modeling medium accompany silver-painted modeled razors.

*W*ashing accessories
The "china" pitcher, basin, and soap dishes are essential to the Victorian doll's toilet. Shaped self-hardening clay is gaily painted and used to house balls of soap.

*H*ot water bottles
Made of modeling medium, the delineated patterns are incised with a sharp tool before baking.

*W*all and shaving mirrors
Real mirror has shells stuck to it for a decorative border. Foil makes a mirrored front to a metal blazer button fixed to a cardboard base.

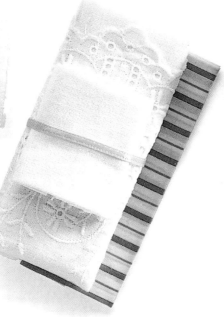

*L*inens and towel rack
Remnants of terry toweling, broderie anglaise, and striped sheeting are used to suggest their real-life cousins. Thin strips of ribbon duplicate the niceties of items stored in Victorian linen cupboards. The towel rack is constructed from templates shown on page 70.

THE VICTORIAN
Bathroom Furniture

SMALL SQUARE TABLE

A match to the one found in the sitting room, this small table can be used to hold guests' soaps and towels or assorted reading material. Instructions and templates for table are on page 80.

Modeling medium African violets in self-hardening clay pots

FABRIC SCREEN

To ensure modesty, lengths of fabric, stiffened with wallpaper paste, are gathered within wood strips. Full making-up instructions on page 80.

Rub-down transfer provides gold-leaf ornamentation

Fabric is pleated and stiffened with wallpaper paste

PLANT STAND

Ideal for holding indoor plants, the instructions and templates for making this unit with integral shelf are on page 70.

Doily cut from lacy material

Pitcher and bowl of self-hardening clay

WOODEN WASHSTAND

Created from wood strip and stained the appropriate color, this has bead handles and a transfer decoration. Glue the 3 x 1⁹/₁₆ in (75 x 40 mm) back between two 4 in (10 cm) pieces of ¹/₄ in (6 mm) squared strip. Cut two 2 ⁹/₁₆ in (65 mm) pieces of squared strip for front legs. Attach two ⁷/₈ x ³/₈ in (22 x 10 mm) side-pieces cut from wood strip between the front and back legs. Add the front ¹/₄ in (6 mm) wide strip between the two front legs and attach two smaller "drawer" fronts. Cut a 1¹/₄ x 3¹/₈ in (34 x 80 mm) bottom shelf, notching the corners. Glue to bottom legs. Add a 1⁹/₁₆ x 3⁵/₁₆ in (40 x 85 mm) top, cutting a square piece out of both back corners to fit between back legs. Add transfer decoration and bead knobs.

*"Relief"
decoration
is painted
lace*

LINEN CUPBOARD

A variation of the wardrobe on page 40, this 4 x 6 x 1½ in (10 x 15 x 4 cm) rectanglar cupboard is constructed from 2 sides, a back, and a top of wood strip. Adapt the templates on page 74 but use the door pattern found on page 75. Strips of clear plastic are attached behind the wooden frame to form the "glass" front. There are four interior shelves; the bottom one forms the base. The top three are covered in paper. Brass hinges, cut from gold tape, and gold beads provide the trim. The top has a decorative curved molding, roughly cut from wood then shaped by sandpaper wrapped around a pencil. All visible pieces are stained.

CISTERN AND TOILET

The toilet, made from self-hardening clay painted with white acrylic, is decorated with "stenciling" and has a wooden-effect clay seat. It is attached to the cistern by means of a white-painted dowel, which is fixed to it with a wad of plastic adhesive. The cistern, a 1 x 1⁹/₁₆ x ⁷/₈ in (25 x 40 x 23 mm) white-painted wooden rectangle has a lace "relief" trim.

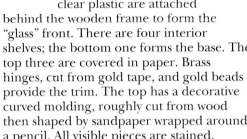

Wooden toilet seat is self-hardening clay painted brown

Head and shoulders only need to be modeled

Linens and towels are miniature versions of the real thing

WASH BASIN

To match the rest of the sanitary ware, this pedestal wash basin, made from self-hardening clay, is heavily stenciled and has "brass" faucets made from modeling medium. It has a tiny modeled plug, which is used to stop up the gold-painted drain, and it is fitted to a freely movable thin chain.

Jewelry chain holds modeled plug

FOOTED BATH

Made of self-hardening clay, this ample bath has a white acrylic paint finish, "brass" modeling medium faucets and a "stenciled" trim. A modeled plug is attached to a thin chain to keep the tub filled with water.

THE MODERN
ℬATHROOM

Smaller, warmer, and more efficient than its Victorian counterpart,
the bathroom of today's modern doll contains numerous electrical aids to
beauty, as well as a wealth of boxed and bottled items that contribute to
personal care. One result of modern plumbing expertise is that the old washstand
with its china bowls and pitcher have been replaced by a modern
sink with hot and cold running water, and the cast iron bath has
been superseded by a pulsating shower unit in
curtained ceramic stall. They may be less
impressive visually, but certainly
more hygienic.

Toilet rolls
Pastel-shaded
papers are cut from
paper tissues and
wound on drinking straw
cores. Painted wood and
metal wire form the holder.

Electrical beauty aids
Portable hair dryers, heated
curlers, and an electric razor
are some modern modeled
essentials.

Towels
An assortment of bath
and hand towels are
created from remnants of
fine terry toweling – the type
used for baby stretch suits. They
are dyed in a small batch of food coloring.
The modern towel rail is fixed to the wall, not
free-standing, and is made of white-painted wood
and thin dowel.

Hot water bottle
This modeled
rectangle has a felt-tip
pattened fabric
covering and a
modeled leak-proof
stopper and neck.

Essential make-up
A tiny zippered pouch
contains a supply of modeled
lipsticks, nail polish, and
mascara, and bead eye
shadow.

Hair care items
Brushes, combs, and head
bands can be stored in the
basket when not in use. All are
made from modeling
medium.

Bath-time toys
A school of fish, a trio of ducks,
and a simple tug are fashioned
out of modeling medium.

*T*ooth care A set of brushes – one for each member of the family, a mug, and tooth paste are all created from modeling medium.

*B*athroom scale Two modeled rectangles of differing sizes are glued one on top of the other. The calibrations can be inked in or cut from paper and covered with a circle of plastic. For comfort, felt fabric is glued to the top.

*B*ath sponges Both natural and artificial sponges are cut to form appropriate shapes. The "loofah" has threads attached to enable its user to apply it to those hard-to-get-at places.

*A*ssorted soaps Plain beauty bars, small guests' soaps, and soaps on a rope are modern-day essentials. Modeling medium and thread are all that is needed.

En Suite Shower Room

Where space is a problem, a shower room often can be installed where a full-sized bathroom won't fit. As long as a toilet can be sited elsewhere, sanitary regulations won't prevent the shower and sink-and-storage unit being fitted into the master bedroom.

*A*ccessories shelf A wooden unit stores the perfumes, creams, lotions, and paper products preferred by today's doll. Most items are modeled.

*C*over and mat set Stretchable terry toweling fabric, in a coordinating shade to the towels, is used for the three-piece suite. The choice of today's modern home-maker, this consists of a toilet lid cover, cut-to-fit toilet mat, and bath mat.

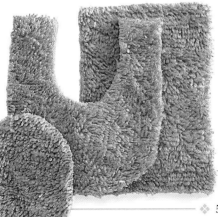

THE VICTORIAN

SITTING ROOM

This, the grandest room in the house, must also be a model of comfort and relaxed domesticity. Papa retreats here when he wants to leave the hustle and bustle of family life behind.

The decor is somewhat formal – no expense has been spared for the elegant striped wallpaper, pelmeted drapes, and needlepoint carpets. Hanging pictures on a ribbon band, such as the flower prints displayed here, is a popular decorative device.

The furniture is also substantial. The glass-fronted cabinet contains ornaments off-limits to children. The green-seated side chair and the desk and matching chair are of good sturdy oak. More lavish are the fringed velvet settee and brocade wing chair.

A number of accessories also attest to the relative prosperity of the inhabitants: the Staffordshire dogs, antique china wall plates, corner collection of "Moss ware", and the variety of gilt-framed oil paintings. In keeping with nineteenth-century convention, Mama has placed all her "best" items here to impress her visitors.

Comfort has been catered for with the satin scatter cushions plumped up on the settee, the needlepointed footstool, the smokers' accessories, and the welcoming display of fresh fruits and sugared plums in their milk glass bowls on their circular table.

Mama's touch is clearly apparent in the selection of fresh flowers and plants scattered throughout the room. The potpourri on the crocheted tablecloth helps to dispel the fumes of any of Papa's cigar-smoking friends.

Ancestral portraits are real photographs cut down and placed in braided frames

Garden roses of modeling medium are freshly gathered in modeled jug

Velvet drapes are fixed to a cardboard pelmet covered with fringe

Framed prints can be easily reproduced using stamps and mitered wooden pieces. Full directions are given on page 13

Potted plants are easily made from masking tape and wire. Follow the directions on page 9

Ornamental china made of self-hardening clay is easy to create; see page 11

Petit point rug is quickly stitched using a rectangle of canvas and silken or cotton threads

Papa's corner
Although Moma had a free hand with the rest of the room, Papa insisted on having his old desk and smoking paraphernalia near at hand in the sitting room.

THE VICTORIAN
SITTING ROOM CATALOG

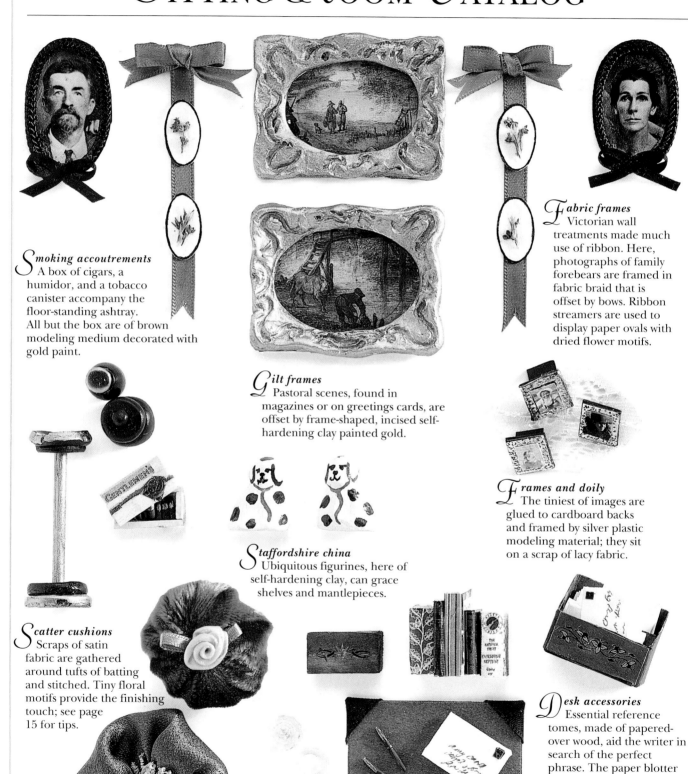

Smoking accoutrements
A box of cigars, a humidor, and a tobacco canister accompany the floor-standing ashtray. All but the box are of brown modeling medium decorated with gold paint.

Gilt frames
Pastoral scenes, found in magazines or on greetings cards, are offset by frame-shaped, incised self-hardening clay painted gold.

Staffordshire china
Ubiquitous figurines, here of self-hardening clay, can grace shelves and mantlepieces.

Fabric frames
Victorian wall treatments made much use of ribbon. Here, photographs of family forebears are framed in fabric braid that is offset by bows. Ribbon streamers are used to display paper ovals with dried flower motifs.

Frames and doily
The tiniest of images are glued to cardboard backs and framed by silver plastic modeling material; they sit on a scrap of lacy fabric.

Scatter cushions
Scraps of satin fabric are gathered around tufts of batting and stitched. Tiny floral motifs provide the finishing touch; see page 15 for tips.

Desk accessories
Essential reference tomes, made of papered-over wood, aid the writer in search of the perfect phrase. The paper blotter has ribbon corners, the pens are modeled, the stamp box is wood and the letter file is paper.

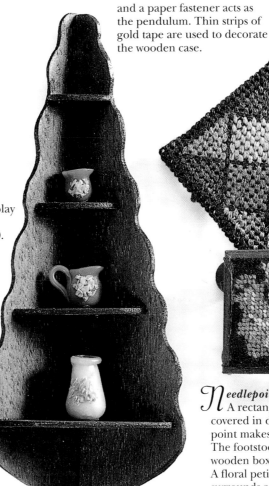

***F**ruits and chocolates*
Sugar-coated plums, fresh fruit in a basket, and boxed chocolates are of modeling medium and paper.

***D**ecorative plates*
Self-hardening clay is shaped into circles and then gaily painted in patterns reminiscent of the 18th century. Then, as now, they were used to decorate walls. See page 11 for how-to.

***B**utterfly collection*
Framed in stained and varnished wood, the paper insects, carefully cut from a magazine advertisement, are a lepidopterist's delight.

***W**all clock*
A button forms the face and a paper fastener acts as the pendulum. Thin strips of gold tape are used to decorate the wooden case.

***P**lants and flowers*
Masking tape and garden wire aspidistra, and dried and modeled flowers are displayed in a cloisonné bead vase.

***W**ooden whatnot*
Instructions and templates for this decorative corner display unit with triangular shelves are on page 80. The "Moss ware" is porcelain modeling medium.

***R**oses*
Modeled blooms on garden wire stalks repose in modeled basket near potpourri petals.

***N**eedlepoint items*
A rectangle of canvas covered in diamonds of petit point makes the ideal carpet. The footstool is a rectangular wooden box on bead feet. A floral petit point cover surrounds a pillow of batting that fits the frame.

THE VICTORIAN
SITTING ROOM FURNITURE

CIRCULAR TABLE This cardboard table is constructed exactly the same as its full-size cousins. Full making-up instructions on page 72.

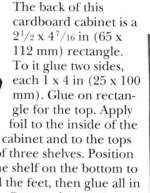

Sturdy velvet fabric topped with lace provides appropriate period feel

Carefully carved fretwork pattern

"Mirrored" shelves and sides created by foil

CURIO CABINET

The back of this cardboard cabinet is a $2^1/_2$ x $4^7/_{16}$ in (65 x 112 mm) rectangle. To it glue two sides, each 1 x 4 in (25 x 100 mm). Glue on rectangle for the top. Apply foil to the inside of the cabinet and to the tops of three shelves. Position one shelf on the bottom to hold the feet, then glue all in place. Cut two doors using the template on page 75. Attach doors with masking tape "hinges" on the inside; add bead knobs, and four $^1/_4$ in (6 mm) lengths of squared strip for the legs.

Knobs are iridescent beads

WING-BACK CHAIR

Deeply padded seat, back, and arms covered in hard-wearing floral print offers durable comfort. Templates and instructions are on page 70.

Create legs from modeling medium

OCCASIONAL CHAIR

This is simple to construct out of cardboard, modeling medium, batting, and fabric. For the seat, form a cardboard rectangular box, 2 in (50 mm) at the front tapering to $1^3/_4$ in (45 mm) at the rear, $1^1/_2$ in (40 mm) deep and with $^1/_2$ in (12 mm) sides. Add batting to top, then cover with fabric, tucking in ends. Cover another piece of cardboard, the same dimensions as the seat top, with fabric and glue to bottom of seat to neaten bottom and provide a base for legs.

Cut a rectangular back $2^1/_2$ x $1^1/_2$ in (65 x 40 mm). Cover the front with batting and then fabric. Glue the padded side of the back to the seat. Apply ribbon along the seat edge and add four modeled legs.

WOODEN DESK

Essential for holding all the important family papers, this is easy to make out of wood strip, single-ply plywood, and gold-headed pins. Cut the back, a 5 x 2 $^9/_{16}$ in (125 x 65 mm) rectangle, and two interior drawer sides, 2 $^3/_8$ x 2 $^9/_{16}$ in (60 x 65 mm) rectangles, out of plywood. Cut two exterior drawer sides, a 5 x 2 $^3/_8$ in (125 x 62 mm) top, and two 1 $^1/_2$ x 2 $^5/_8$ in (38 x 67 mm) fronts out of woodstrip. Stain all pieces as desired. When dry, rough assemble and then glue the two exterior sides to the back. Carefully position the two interior sides and glue these to the back, then add the fronts and top. Cut six $^5/_{16}$ x 1 $^3/_{16}$ in (15 x 30 mm) drawer fronts out of wood strip and glue three to each front. Push pins through the wood to form knobs.

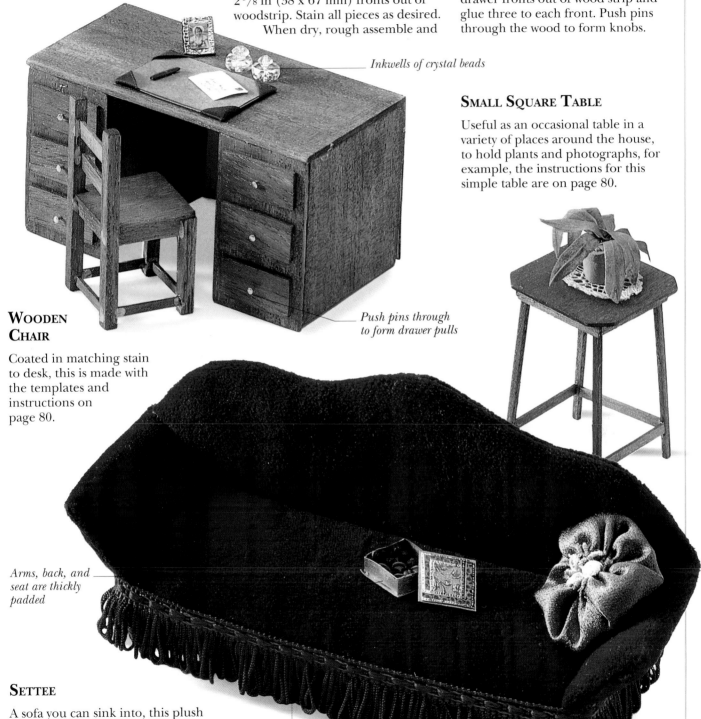

Inkwells of crystal beads

Push pins through to form drawer pulls

SMALL SQUARE TABLE

Useful as an occasional table in a variety of places around the house, to hold plants and photographs, for example, the instructions for this simple table are on page 80.

WOODEN CHAIR

Coated in matching stain to desk, this is made with the templates and instructions on page 80.

Arms, back, and seat are thickly padded

SETTEE

A sofa you can sink into, this plush piece of furniture takes pride of place in any sitting room. The fringed trim and beaded feet are in proper period style. Full making-up instructions are on page 71.

Chocolates of modeling medium nestle in gilt-paper covered box

THE 1930'S
Living Room

The decorator planning to recreate this look should bear in mind the influences on the period – which were new directions in design and a stagnating economy. Art Deco designers favored geometric detailing on wood, the malleable properties of plastic, and bright patterns on ceramics. The economies of the period meant that hand-knitted and embroidered goods often had to take the place of commercially produced ones.

Gift parcels
Filled with hand-knitted socks and gloves these paper-wrapped wood boxes are tied with thread twine.

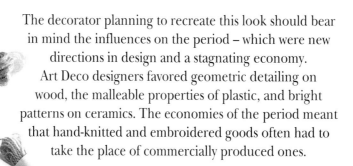

Susie Cooper tea set
Teapot, cups and saucers, sugar bowl, and milk jug are made of self-hardening clay. See page 11 for tips on making.

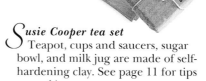

Knitting accessories
Cocktail-stick needles with bead handles are used to knit skeins of embroidery-thread yarn. The needles and yarn are kept safe from prying hands in embroidered felt carryalls.

Photograph album
Paper leaves hold "photographs" of relatives past and present cut from stamps, magazines, and catalogs. The "leatherbound" cover is made of cardboard trimmed with paper.

Home sweet home
Embroidered picture is done in diagonal stitch with single thread on petit point canvas. See page 13 for framing tips.

Deco clock
Graduated rectangles of wood strip are glued to a central block. The face is from a magazine.

Thirties plates
Self-hardening clay plates are painted with period decoration. See page 11 for how-to.

Domestic Bliss

A haven against growing monetary and political problems, the '30s living room epitomizes comfortable domesticity. Thoughts of relatives are ever present, witness the gift parcels ready for posting and the well thumbed family photograph album. The radio is a constant companion along with one's knitting, and there is always the dessert cart when worries become too pressing.

Thirties radios

The "carved wood" cardboard facades fit over mesh "speakers" and plastic tuning bands. "Bakelite" knobs are beads.

Pipes and tobacco

Carved wooden pipe-rack supports a selection while the felt tobacco pouch holds a pinch of the real thing. Cocktail-stick cleaners, painted white, are on hand to clear any obstructions.

Magazine rack

Made from cardboard it holds various publications of paper, or wood blocks covered in printed illustrations.

Comfy cushions

Made for use on floors and sofas, squares of plain and plush material are filled with millet or other seeds. Alternatively, plain fabric can be decorated with embroidered flowers and trimmed in chain stitch before filling.

Decorative "barbola" mirror

Plasticized foil has cardboard backing and painted modeled trim. It hangs by jewelry chain.

THE FAMILY

An entire family of dolls can be created simply from modeling medium; pipe cleaners; surgical tape; strong, clear adhesive, and fabric. The head and limbs are modeled then baked according to the manufacturer's instructions. When dry, the body is assembled and can be clothed. Add a few sprigs of lavender to make them scented. Faces can be modeled as desired. Facial features are painted on and may require some practice on paper before you become proficient. With brown paint make the eyebrows and outline the eyes. When dry, add irises then touches of white for the corner, and finally add further brown for eyelashes and to accentuate any features. Paint mouth red or pink.

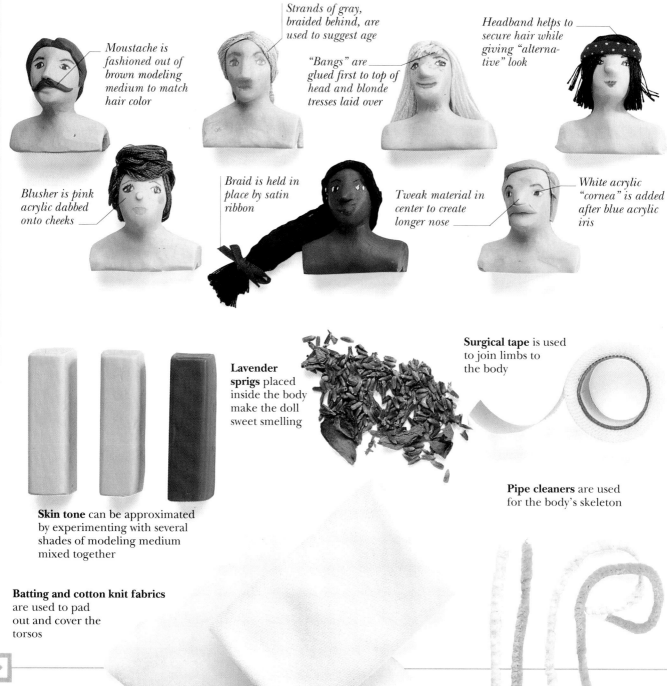

Moustache is fashioned out of brown modeling medium to match hair color

Strands of gray, braided behind, are used to suggest age

"Bangs" are glued first to top of head and blonde tresses laid over

Headband helps to secure hair while giving "alternative" look

Blusher is pink acrylic dabbed onto cheeks

Braid is held in place by satin ribbon

Tweak material in center to create longer nose

White acrylic "cornea" is added after blue acrylic iris

Lavender sprigs placed inside the body make the doll sweet smelling

Surgical tape is used to join limbs to the body

Skin tone can be approximated by experimenting with several shades of modeling medium mixed together

Pipe cleaners are used for the body's skeleton

Batting and cotton knit fabrics are used to pad out and cover the torsos

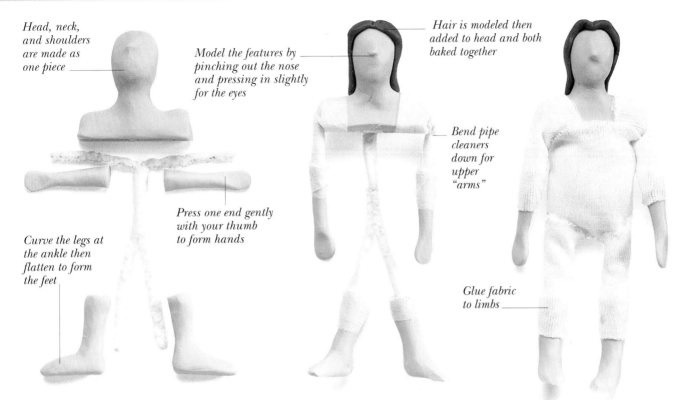

Head, neck, and shoulders are made as one piece

Model the features by pinching out the nose and pressing in slightly for the eyes

Hair is modeled then added to head and both baked together

Bend pipe cleaners down for upper "arms"

Press one end gently with your thumb to form hands

Curve the legs at the ankle then flatten to form the feet

Glue fabric to limbs

MAKE THE HEAD AND BODY

Take a 1 in (2.5 cm) diameter ball of modeling medium, mixed to the appropriate shade, and create the head, neck, and shoulders. Model the features as desired. Square the shoulders and press them against a dowel to create a channel underneath.

Roll out modeling medium into thin sausage shapes for arms and thicker ones for legs.

Take 2 pipe cleaners and join with a piece of tape; flatten the tops.

ASSEMBLE THE PIECES

Bake the modeled pieces according to manufacturer's directions. If you are adding modeled hair, apply this to the baked head and then bake again. If you plan to use thread, see below.

Using clear adhesive, attach the pipe cleaners to the channel underneath the shoulders; secure with surgical tape. Then tape the legs and arms onto the pipe cleaners.

FINISH THE BODY

Pad the torso slightly with batting and a few sprigs of lavender, if you like. Then cover the "skeleton" with knit fabric, cutting it to size. Use glue to attach fabric to the modeled limbs and stitch where fabric pieces meet.

Threaded Hair

Embroidery thread in varying shades can be used for hair. This is applied after the doll is finished. Take the shade of your choice and wrap it approximately 10 times around your fingers – two for short hair, three for longer, etc. Using the same shade, work across the hair in chain stitch, joining all the strands. When secured, cut the end. With the stitching in the middle, glue the hair to the top of the head. You can add bangs or braid the strands for different effects.

DRESSING THE FAMILY

While it is perfectly possible to make clothes from patterns, the simplest and most effective way of dressing the family is to cut scraps of fabric and, using a strong clear adhesive, glue them directly to the doll. Solids or small print fabrics work best. To prevent the edges of certain materials unraveling, use a commercially available fray preventer or clear nail polish. Materials should be made of natural fibers as these drape more readily and effectively than polyesters or acrylics.

Hair and earrings are glued to the head, if not modeled, and shoes can be painted on the feet, if desired.

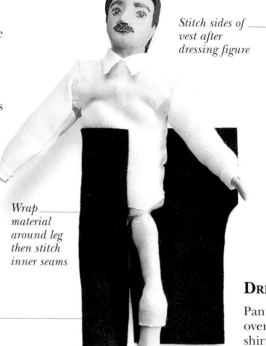

Stitch sides of vest after dressing figure

Wrap material around leg then stitch inner seams

Pants and vest are simple shapes that are tailored to fit and then glued

DRESSING A WOMAN

Normally, attire is made up of several pieces. A petticoat, of broderie anglaise, is made first and applied directly over the integral underwear. Then the sleeves and bodice of the dress are attached, followed by the gathered skirt. Finally lace or other trim is added.

DRESSING A MAN

Pants and tops are applied directly over integral long johns. While the shirt consists of a separate back, front, and sleeves, the vest and flannel pants are both cleverly cut from one piece of fabric. The pants are wrapped around the legs and the inner seams are stitched. The vest is placed over the head and the outer seams are stitched.

Dress is made in several pieces. The sleeves and back are attached first, then the gathered skirt, and finally the front with lace collar is added. The petticoat, of broderie anglaise, was made first

Trims neaten and adorn garments

A single garment may be made up of a number of pieces

COSTUME GALLERY

Hair is modeled and the moustache and shoes painted on afterwards

Babies wear diapers of terry toweling and christening dress of lace fabric over white satin

Victorian housemaid sports an apron and cap over everyday shift of striped fabric

Victorian man wears satin smoking jacket and cravat with cotton pants

Victorian woman wears a frock of satin trimmed with plaid. Her hat is made from a matching fabric scrap and feather

Earrings are tiny jewelry findings glued to her head

Girl wears small print dress with pinafore of lacy material. Her strappy shoes are painted on

Country woman is dressed in calico dress with homespun apron on top. Her straw hat is made from braided threads

Teenager is dressed in knitted top and corduroy pants

Adolescent boy with freckle-fresh face sports woven jeans and checked shirt

USING THE TEMPLATES

The templates will produce furniture that is of $^1/_{12}$th scale. Do not cut the templates from the book but use tracing paper to create a paper template and transfer this to wood or cardboard. Be careful to transfer the score lines properly; a straight edge will come in handy. It is recommended to rough assemble all pieces first to make sure of fit, so that if anything isn't exact you can adjust for it before glueing. Remember, too, to stain any wood pieces before you apply the glue.

Occasionally you may want to enlarge a template to suit a doll larger than the $^1/_{12}$th size, a model doll, for example. Or, you may want to reduce a larger pattern, found in another book, for use in your dollhouse. The instructions given on the opposite page are easy to follow but a good result depends upon accurate measuring and correct positioning.

To reduce a larger pattern or template, follow the procedure for enlarging but reverse the process so you work from the greater measure to the lesser.

You will find the necessary instructions to complete each item near its set of templates. In addition to the list of supplies given, scissors or a craft knife will be needed to cut (and score) the templates.

Some of the templates need to be used more than once in constructing a particular item, and will be marked "Cut 2", for example.

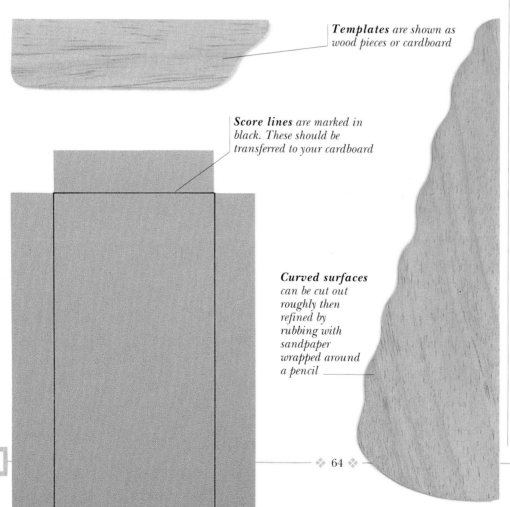

Templates *are shown as wood pieces or cardboard*

Score lines *are marked in black. These should be transferred to your cardboard*

Curved surfaces *can be cut out roughly then refined by rubbing with sandpaper wrapped around a pencil*

ENLARGING A TEMPLATE

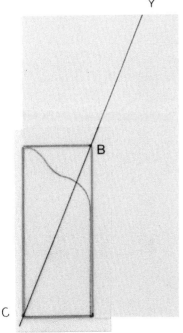

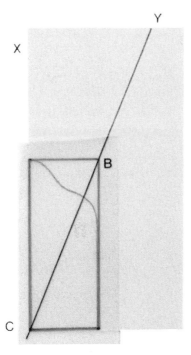

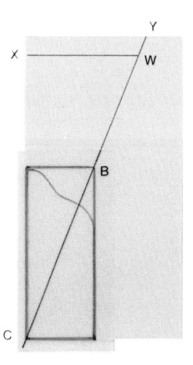

1 ~ Trace the template and draw a rectangle around it. Then take a large piece of paper and lay the traced template at the corner of it. Draw a line from the bottom left (C) through the top right (B) and onwards to the the larger piece (Y).

2 ~ Determine the desired height of the enlargement by working upwards from the bottom left (C) and to your chosen point. Mark this with an X.

3 ~ Draw a horizontal line from the point (X) of the larger paper through line CBY to (W), the right-hand point, making sure it is parallel to the base.

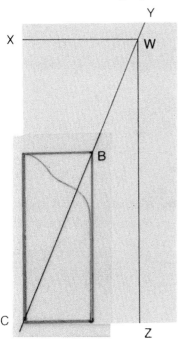

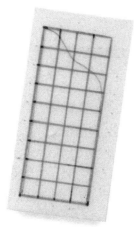

4 ~ Complete the new outline by drawing a vertical line from the top right-hand point (W) to the base (Z).

5 ~ Divide the original template and the new outline into the same number of squares. Draw the template freehand, square by square, on the new outline with its proportionally larger squares, using a ruler for a straight edge.

DRESSING TABLE

You will need ~

Traces of 2 templates
Cardboard
Tape
Fabric
Glue
Lace trim
Decorative ribbon

1 ~ Transfer template traces to cardboard. For pedestal bases, score along black lines and fold into rectangles, holding the corners together with tape.

2 ~ Cover with fabric, stuck on with glue. Add lace trim to the bottom of each base.

3 ~ For table top, score along black lines and fold; tape the corners.

4 ~ Cover with fabric then apply lace all around the perimeter of the top. Add decorative ribbon trim around edges.

5 ~ Using glue, attach the pedestals to the table top.

**Pedestal base
Cut 2**

Fold along lines

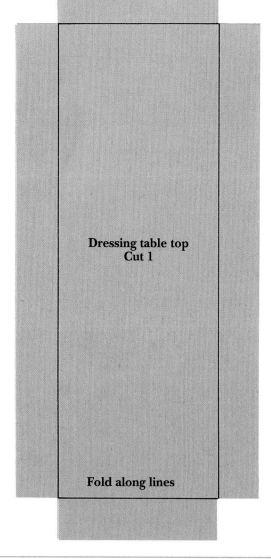

**Dressing table top
Cut 1**

Fold along lines

PAIL

You will need ~

Traces of 2 templates
Paper
Glue
Silver paint
Wire

1 ~ Transfer the traces to paper and assemble the pail by wrapping the larger piece onto itself so that the 2 handle supports are opposite each other. Glue the join.

2 ~ Push the bottom piece inside and paint the pail with silver.

3 ~ Thread wire through hole in each handle support; bend the end up.

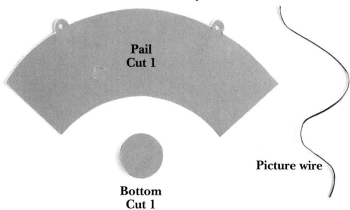

**Pail
Cut 1**

Picture wire

**Bottom
Cut 1**

SHELF

You will need ~
Traces of 3 templates
Wood strip
Tea for stain, optional
Masking tape
Glue

1 ~ Transfer traces of templates to wood strip and cut out the back piece, two sides, and three shelves.

2 ~ For "pine" effect, stain with tea, 2 or 3 coats may be necessary.

3 ~ Glue the side pieces to the back and position the shelves, using masking tape, to check fit.

4 ~ When you are happy with the fit, glue the shelves to the sides and back.

Shelf back
Cut 1

Shelf side
Cut 2

Shelves
Cut 3

BATHTUB RACK

Side Cut 2

You will need ~
Traces of 3 templates
Wood strip
Glue

Side
Cut 2

Top
Cut 1

1 ~ Transfer traces of templates to wood and cut top and 4 sides. Use emery board or sandpaper wrapped around a pencil to neaten curves.

2 ~ Glue sides together then attach top.

SERVING TROLLEY

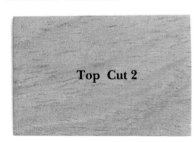

Top Cut 2

Side Cut 4

Paper fastener

Side Cut 4

You will need ~
Traces of 1 template
Squared strip
Wood strip
Wood stain
Glue
4 paper fasteners

1 ~ Transfer trace to wood strip and cut out 2 tops.

2 ~ Out of squared strip cut 8 sides to lengths shown. Cut 4 legs ¼ in (6 mm) longer than longest side.

3 ~ Stain all pieces; when dry, glue sides to tops and then glue legs.

4 ~ Remove one end of fasteners, leaving head for wheel and push other end into bottom of leg.

SEWING BOX

You will need ~
Traces of 6 templates
Wood strip
Squared strip
Stain
Glue
Lace
Brown paper

1 ~ Transfer traced templates to wood and cut top, base, cross piece, 2 legs, and 4 sides. Cut 4 feet and 2 supports from squared strip to lengths shown. Cut 4 dividers from brown paper.

2 ~ With sandpaper wrapped round a pencil, smooth the curves in the legs. Trim the perimeter of the box with a strip of lace cut to size and stain along with wood.

3 ~ When pieces are dry, join the sides to the underneath of the base and glue on the supports. Then add the legs and graduated feet. Slot in the cross piece at the bottom between the graduated feet.

4 ~ Cut notches in the paper dividers at one-third and two-thirds along their lengths and fit together to form nine compartments.

5 ~ If you like, you can decorate the top of the box.

Side
Cut 4

Base
Cut 1

Divider Cut 4

Cross piece
Cut 1

Leg
Cut 2

Sewing box top
Cut 1

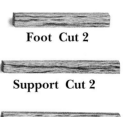

Foot Cut 2

Support Cut 2

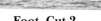

Foot Cut 2

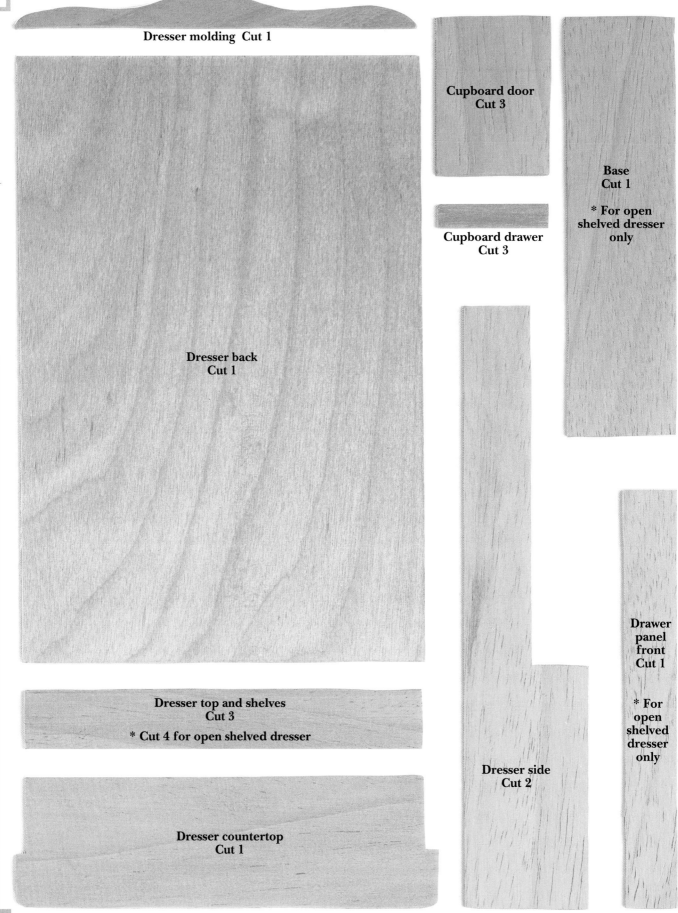

Dresser molding Cut 1

**Cupboard door
Cut 3**

**Cupboard drawer
Cut 3**

**Base
Cut 1**

*** For open
shelved dresser
only**

**Dresser back
Cut 1**

**Drawer
panel
front
Cut 1**

*** For
open
shelved
dresser
only**

**Dresser top and shelves
Cut 3**

* Cut 4 for open shelved dresser

**Dresser side
Cut 2**

**Dresser countertop
Cut 1**

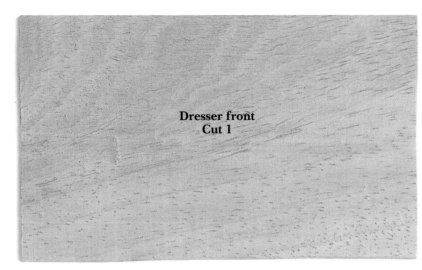

**Dresser front
Cut 1**

WELSH DRESSER

You will need ~
*Traces of 8 templates
Wood strip
Single-ply plywood
Masking tape
Glue
Modeling medium
Tea for stain, optional*

1 ~ Transfer traces of template shapes for the 2 sides, 2 shelves and top, countertop, 3 cupboard doors, 3 drawers, curved molding, and front to the wood strip. Cut out shapes. Cut out back from plywood.

2 ~ Using masking tape, rough assemble the major pieces – the two sides to the back, and the front to the sides. Slot in the shelves and the top and countertop.

3 ~ When you are happy with the fit, if you like, remove the tape and stain all the pieces with strong tea, 2 or 3 coats may be necessary.

4 ~ When the pieces are dry, glue all pieces together adding the curved molding, the cupboard doors, and the drawer fronts.

5 ~ Glue on knobs of shaped modeling material.

MODESTY SCREEN

You will need ~
*Trace of 1
    template
Wood strip
Wood stain
4 rub-down
    transfers
Masking tape*

1 ~ Transfer trace of template to wood strip and cut out 4 panels. If desired, stain.

2 ~ When dry, apply transfer to each panel. Use masking tape to hold panels together.

**Panel
Cut 4**

SMALL RECTANGULAR TABLE

You will need ~
*Traces of 4
    templates
Squared strip
Wood strip
Tea for stain,
    optional
Glue
Modeling
    medium or
    bead for knob*

1 ~ Transfer traced templates to wood strip and cut 1 top, 4 sides and a drawer front. Cut 4 pieces of squared strip to length shown for legs. Stain pieces with tea before glueing, if desired.

2 ~ Glue the two long and two short sides together to form a rectangular support

for the top. Glue the top to the support.

3 ~ Carefully glue one leg into each corner.

4 ~ Add the drawer front and glue on a knob of modeling medium, painted, if necessary, or small bead.

**Table top
Cut 1**

**Table side
Cut 2**

**Table side
Cut 2**

**Table drawer
Cut 1**

**Table leg
Cut 4**

PLANT STAND

You will need ~
Traces of 3 templates
Wood strip
Squared strip
Glue
Wood stain

1 ~ Transfer traces and cut top, shelf, and 4 sides from wood strip. Smooth ends with sandpaper wrapped around a pencil.

2 ~ Cut 4 legs from squared strip to length shown. Stain all pieces as desired.

3 ~ When the pieces are dry, glue the sides underneath the top then glue each leg into a corner. Add the shelf approximately two-thirds the way down the legs.

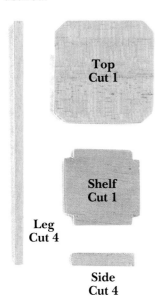

Top Cut 1

Shelf Cut 1

Leg Cut 4

Side Cut 4

TOWEL RAIL

You will need ~
Traces of 1 template
Wood strip
Wood stain
Dowel
Glue

1 ~ Transfer trace of side to wood strip and cut out.

2 ~ If edges are rough, take a piece of sandpaper, wrap it around a pencil, and use this to finely shape the curved edges.

3 ~ Cut 4 pieces of dowel to the length shown for rails; sand the edges neatly.

4 ~ Apply stain and when dry, glue dowels in place, one along the bottom, one on top, and two opposing just beneath.

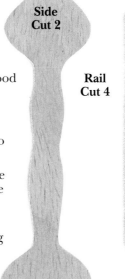

Side Cut 2

Rail Cut 4

WING-BACK CHAIR

You will need ~
Traces of 3 templates
Cardboard
Batting
Glue
Fabric
Masking tape
Rubber band
Modeling medium
  or beads

1 ~ Transfer traces to cardboard and cut out 2 chair backs, making one slightly smaller than the other, 2 seats and a front.

2 ~ Score the larger chair back along black lines and bend forward.

3 ~ Using the back template, cut a piece of batting 1 in (2.5 cm) larger all around. Glue batting to the back, trimming it at the top but wrapping excess over chair "arms".

4 ~ Again, using the back template, cut out your chosen upholstery fabric, adding 1 in (2.5 cm) all around and use this to cover the batting.

5 ~ Score the smaller back piece along black lines and bend slightly forward. Cover it in fabric. Right side facing outward, glue this back to the first one, making sure any excess fabric is well tucked in between the two.

6 ~ Cover one seat with batting and fabric, tucking ends under and glueing.

7 ~ Cover the front piece with some batting and fabric.

8 ~ Cover the other seat piece with fabric. Sandwich the front between both seats, the padded one on top, and glue together. Apply glue around sides and back of seat and slot into back. Hold all pieces together with a rubber band until the glue sets.

9 ~ Make legs of modeling medium or use wooden beads. Attach to base.

Chair back Cut 2

Fold along lines

Chair seat Cut 2

Chair front Cut 1

SETTEE

You will need ~

Traces of 3 templates
Cardboard
Tape
Batting
Fabric
Rubber band
Card
Beads
Braid or other trim

1 ~ For the base, transfer the traced template to cardboard and cut out; score along the black lines. Fold the base into a box shape. Use tape to reinforce the corners. Cut a piece of batting to fit the seat area and glue in place. Cover the base with your fabric, as neatly as possible, tucking the edges in well out of sight.

2 ~ To make the back, transfer the traced template to cardboard and cut out two. Use the same template to cut a piece of batting to fit. Glue the batting onto one back. Using the back template but adding 1 in (2.5 cm) all around, cut out 2 pieces of your fabric and use one to cover back. Tuck edges well in. Trim $1/16$ in (2 mm) all around the perimeter of the second back piece and glue on other piece of fabric. Snip away any excess fabric and, keeping the padded side to the front, glue the other back to it, right sides facing outwards.

3 ~ For the arms, transfer the traced template to

cardboard and cut out 2; score along black lines. Glue on some batting. Fold your fabric in half right sides facing and, using the arm template, cut out two coverings, adding $1/2$ in (12 mm) all around. Stitch the fabric on two sides to form a sleeve. Turn right side out and insert the padded arm piece. Sew up the third side.

4 ~ To assemble the settee, fit the base to the back and the arms to the base and back. Take note where surfaces meet and, when you are happy with the shape and fit, apply a thin line of glue along these meeting

places. Press the pieces together firmly, and use your rubber band to hold them in place until the glue has set.

5 ~ To neaten the base, cut a piece of card to the shape and cover it with fabric. Glue it to the bottom of the base. Attach the beads to form a foot on each corner. Apply braid or other trim around edges.

Score along line

**Settee arm
Cut 2**

**Settee back
Cut 2**

Fold along lines

**Settee base
Cut 1**

ROUND TABLE

You will need ~
Traces of 2 templates
Cardboard
Tape
Glue
Fabric

1 ~ Transfer traces to cardboard, making two base pieces, and cut out.

2 ~ Starting at the top of each base, cut out a notch in the center, approximately $^1/_{16}$ in (2 mm) wide and $1^1/_8$ in (30 mm) long, stopping about 1 in (25 mm) from the end.

3 ~ Slot one base into the other forming an intersecting support. If necessary, use tape to strengthen join.

4 ~ Glue circular table top to base. When firmly set, cut out a piece of fabric, 7 in (17.5 cm) in diameter, and attach to the table top. If you like, cover this with a smaller circular lacy piece, approximately $4^1/_4$ in (11 cm) in diameter.

Table top
Cut 1

Table base
Cut 2

Washstand top
Cut 1

Washstand shelf
Cut 1

Overhang
Cut 1

Washstand side
Cut 2

Washstand back
Cut 1

WASHSTAND

You will need ~
Traces of 5 templates
Cardboard
Glue
Acrylic primer and paint

1 ~ Transfer traces to cardboard and cut out 2 sides, back, top, shelf and overhang.

2 ~ Glue sides to back; add top, overhang, and shelf.

3 ~ Cover with primer and then, when dry, paint.

4 ~ Apply paint in blobs to get raised decorative effect for the ends of the overhang and in the middle of the curved back.

SKIRTED CHAIR

You will need ~
Traces of 4 templates
Cardboard
Batting
Glue
Fabric and ribbon trim
Tape

1 ~ Transfer traced templates to cardboard and cut out. Using front template, cut out batting and glue to front. Cover with fabric.

2 ~ Cover the back with fabric and, wrong sides facing, glue the back to the front, making certain any excess fabric is covered.

3 ~ Cut a circle of fabric, 6 in (15 cm) in diameter. If you like, paint the edge with fabric sealer to keep it from fraying.

4 ~ Take the base piece and tape the ends so it makes a 1³/₄ in (45 mm) diameter cylinder.

5 ~ To the chair seat, glue a piece of batting cut to the same size. Fix seat to top of base and glue fabric piece over it so that it drapes.

6 ~ Add ribbon trim along the edge of the seat; glue base piece to chair back.

Chair base
Cut 1

Chair back
Cut 1

Chair seat
Cut 1

Chair front
Cut 1

Finished front

Dollhouse back
Cut 2

Dollhouse base
Cut 1

Dollhouse side
Cut 2

Dollhouse roof and floors
Cut 4

DOLLHOUSE

You will need ~
Traces of 4 templates
Single-ply plywood
Acrylic primer and paint
Glue
Fabric
Beads
Tape

1 ~ Transfer traces of templates to plywood and cut out 2 backs, 2 sides, the roof and 2 floors, and the base. On one back cut out windows and door to make a front.

2 ~ Paint the exterior and interior and glue fabric scraps to "walls", "floors", and "attic ceiling". Attach the sides of the house to the back, and the base to the sides.

3 ~ Glue in the floors and attach the roof pieces.

4 ~ Add any tiny pieces of furniture of painted wood, beads, fabric, or modeling medium to the interior.

5 ~ Paint the front of the house appropriately, picking out window boxes and trailing roses, and when dry, decorate the reverse side, paying particular attention to window treatments.

6 ~ Attach the front with transparent tape "hinges".

Molding Cut 1

**Wardrobe front
Cut 2**

**Wardrobe back
Cut 1**

**Wardrobe side
Cut 3**

WARDROBE

You will need ~
Traces of 6 templates
Cardboard
Glue
Acrylic primer, paint
Tape
Fabric
Dowel

**Wardrobe shelf
Cut 3**

**Wardrobe base and top
Cut 2**

1 ~ Transfer the traces
to cardboard and cut out
back, 3 sides, 2 fronts, top
and base, decorative
molding, and 3 shelves.

2 ~ Glue sides to the back,
and add the top, base, and
molding.

3 ~ Paint this frame and
both sides of the doors with
primer and pink acrylic.

4 ~ When dry, attach the
doors on the inside with
transparent tape.

Hanging rail Cut 1

5 ~ Using a glue stick to
attach the fabric, line the
interior of the wardrobe
and the back of the doors,
covering the transparent
"hinges".

6 ~ Trim $1/16$ in (2 mm) off
long edge of the remaining
side. Cover it and the
shelves in fabric. Glue the
fabric-covered side to the
back of the wardrobe as a

CHEST OF DRAWERS

You will need ~
Traces of 4 templates
Wood strip
Wood stain
8 pearls

1 ~ Transfer traced templates to wood and cut out front, back, 2 sides, top, and 4 drawers.

2 ~ With sandpaper wrapped around a pencil, smooth bottom edge of front; stain pieces as desired.

3 ~ Glue the sides to the back and the front to the sides. Add the top.

4 ~ Starting ⅛ in (4mm) from top, glue on "drawers" ⅛ in (4mm) apart. Add pearls for knobs.

**Chest back and front
Cut 2**

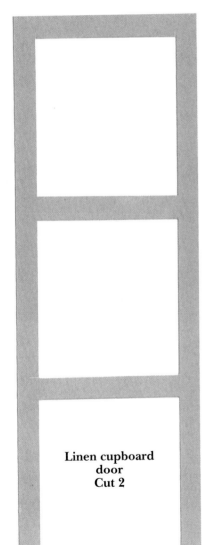

**Linen cupboard
door
Cut 2**

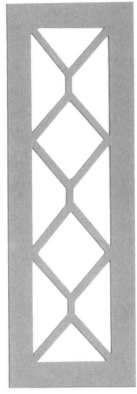

**Curio cabinet door
Cut 2**

**Chest side
Cut 2**

**Chest drawer
Cut 4**

**Chest top
Cut 1**

support for the shelves. Glue in the three shelves.

7 ~ Cut dowel to length shown and glue in ½ in (12 mm) down from top on left side as hanging rail.

8 ~ Paint on further decoration to the front of the wardrobe doors and top molding. A blob of paint should serve as the door knobs.

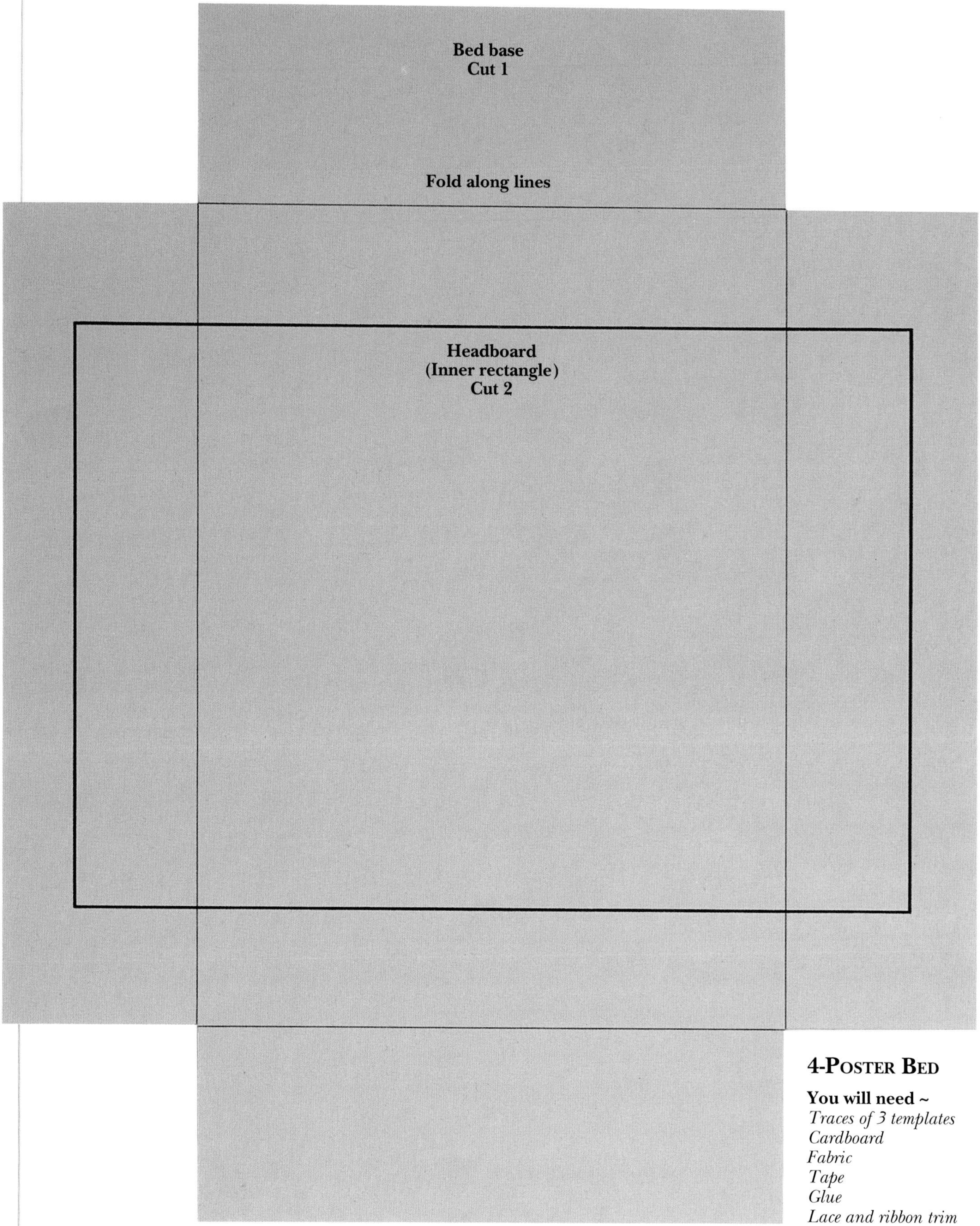

**Bed base
Cut 1**

Fold along lines

**Headboard
(Inner rectangle)
Cut 2**

4-POSTER BED

You will need ~
*Traces of 3 templates
Cardboard
Fabric
Tape
Glue
Lace and ribbon trim
Dowel
Paint*

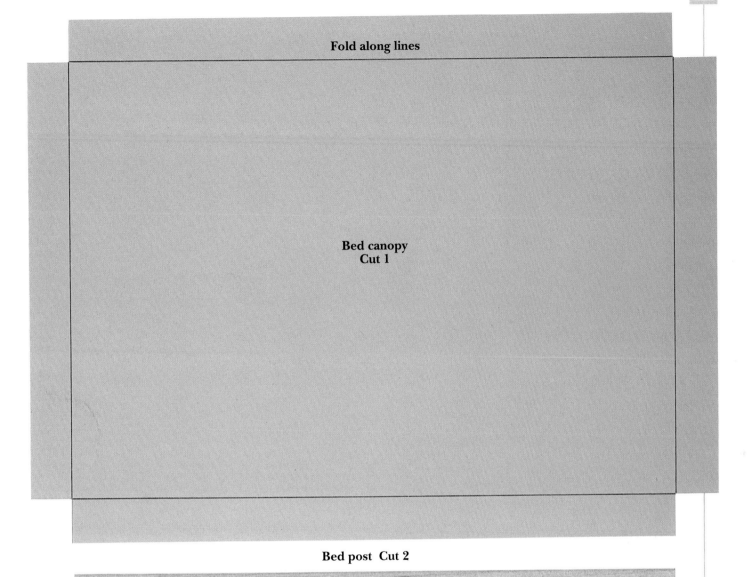

Fold along lines

**Bed canopy
Cut 1**

Bed post Cut 2

Create the Base

1 ~ Transfer larger trace to cardboard. Score along black lines and fold down, holding the corners together with tape.

2 ~ For the "valance": hem one end of a 40 x 4 in (100 x 10 cm) piece of fabric and then gather it at the other end so a ruffled edge is formed. Glue valance to the centre of the base.

3 ~ To hold the valance in place, cut another piece of cardboard, the same size as the top of the base, cover with a matching piece of fabric, and glue it firmly in place over the top.

Make the Headboard

1 ~ Transfer trace to 2 pieces of cardboard. Cover both with fabric.

2 ~ Attach one fabric-covered piece to the top end of the bed's base. Set the other headboard piece aside for later.

Form the Canopy

1 ~ Transfer trace to cardboard. Score along black lines and fold down, holding the corners together with tape.

2 ~ Cover with fabric, tucking the edges in at the corners and glue fabric to underside of canopy.

3 ~ For the frill: hem one end of a 40 x 2 in (100 x 5 cm) piece of fabric and then gather it at the other end so a ruffled edge is formed. Glue this to the inside edge of the canopy so it faces right side out.

4 ~ To neaten the canopy and help hold the frill in place, cut another piece of cardboard, the same size as the top of the canopy, cover with a matching piece of fabric, and glue it firmly in place to the underside.

5 ~ Add a strip of lace all around the underside of the frill. Glue a strip of

embroidered flower trim all around the perimeter of the canopy.

Add the Drapes

1 ~ Cut two pieces of fabric 2 x 7$\frac{1}{2}$ in (5 x 19 cm); make a $\frac{1}{4}$ in (6 mm) hem on all sides and glue lace trim to one long end of each piece.

2 ~ Take the untrimmed long end of each "drape" and glue it to the back of the headboard, about $\frac{1}{4}$ in (6mm) in.

3 ~ Then attach the second fabric-covered headboard piece, right side out, so the drapes are

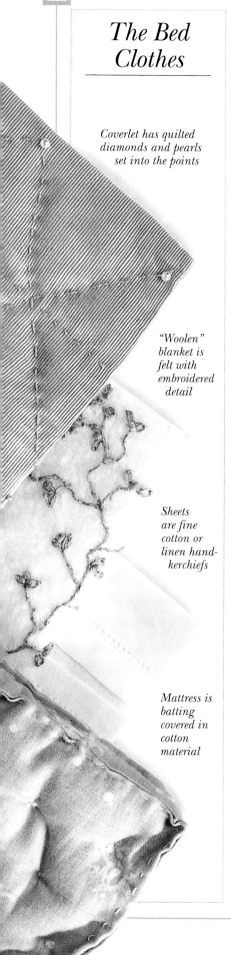

The Bed Clothes

Coverlet has quilted diamonds and pearls set into the points

"Woolen" blanket is felt with embroidered detail

Sheets are fine cotton or linen hand-kerchiefs

Mattress is batting covered in cotton material

carefully and neatly sandwiched between the two headboard pieces.

Assemble the bed

1 ~ Cut 2 bed posts from dowel to length shown. If you like, paint the dowel or cover with fabric or ribbon.

2 ~ Insert the end of each dowel into the bed base (making a slight hole in the fabric) $1/4$ in (6 mm) in from the end of the bed.

3 ~ Set the canopy on top of the dowels and headboard. Glue, if necessary.

KITCHEN STOVE

You will need ~
Traces of 11 templates
Cardboard
Masking tape
Glue
Acrylic primer and black paint
Split peas
Gold paint
Tile-decorated paper
Gold stars
Tissue paper: red, orange, yellow and black

1 ~ Transfer all the template shapes to cardboard. Cut out shapes.

2 ~ Using masking tape, join the major pieces of the stove – the two outer sides to the back, the front to the sides, and the inner sides (at the edge of the "grate" on the front) to the back.

3 ~ Slot in the shelf and top of the stove. Assemble the ash box.

4 ~ When you are happy with the fit, glue the pieces together.

5 ~ Glue on the "oven doors" and "drawers".

6 ~ Paint the entire unit with the black acrylic paint; paint the split peas with gold paint.

7 ~ When the stove is dry, attach the tile-decorated paper to the splashback –

the back and sides of the stove – and the gold split-pea "knobs" to the drawers and doors.

8 ~ Cut 4 "hinges" from gold stars and attach 2 to the outer side of each oven door.

9 ~ Fill the ash box with crumpled tissue paper and tape it to the inner sides so it is held securely.

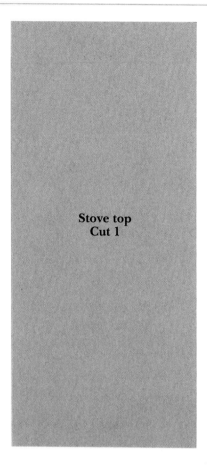

Shelf
Cut 1

Stove top
Cut 1

Ash box side
Cut 2

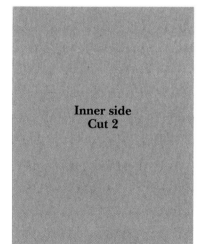

Inner side
Cut 2

Oven drawer Cut 2

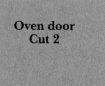

Oven door
Cut 2

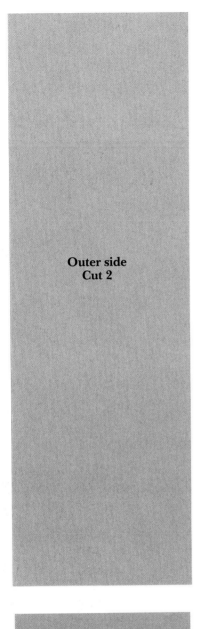

Outer side
Cut 2

Stove back
Cut 1

Ash box base
Cut 1

Ash box side
Cut 2

Stove front
Cut 1

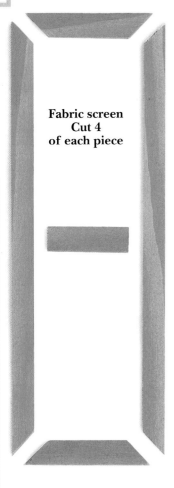

**Fabric screen
Cut 4
of each piece**

CORNER SHELF

You will need ~
*Traces of 5
   templates
Wood strip
Sandpaper
Wood stain
Glue*

FABRIC
SCREEN

You will need ~
*Traces of 5 templates
Wood strip
Glue and wallpaper glue
Fabric
Transparent tape*

1 ~ Transfer traces to wood
and cut out four panels.
Join the pieces to form a
rectangle with central strip.

2 ~ Cut 4 pieces of fabric
the length of each frame
but twice the width.

3 ~ Paint fabric with wallpaper glue and pleat to fit
the frame. Let dry and glue
to back of each frame.

4 ~ Tape along the back to
join frames together.

1 ~ Transfer traces to wood
strip and cut out 2 sides
and 4 shelves.

2 ~ Using sandpaper
wrapped around a pencil,
smooth the curves. Stain
pieces as desired.

3 ~ Glue one side
along the edge of the
other side. Glue in
shelves approximately
1 in (2.5 cm) apart.

**Shelf
Cut 1**

**Shelf
Cut 1**

**Shelf
Cut 1**

**Shelf
Cut 1**

**Corner shelf side
Cut 2**

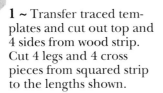

Leg Cut 4

Side piece Cut 4

**Cross piece
Cut 4**

**Square table top
Cut 1**

SMALL SQUARE TABLE

You will need ~
*Traces of 2 templates
Wood strip
Squared strip
Glue
Wood stain*

1 ~ Transfer traced templates and cut out top and
4 sides from wood strip.
Cut 4 legs and 4 cross
pieces from squared strip
to the lengths shown.

2 ~ Stain pieces as desired.

3 ~ Glue sides to underneath of top.

4 ~ Glue a leg in each
corner; glue cross pieces
between the legs.

WOODEN CHAIR

You will need ~
*Traces of 3 templates
Wood strip
Squared strip
Wood stain
Glue*

1 ~ Transfer traces to
wood strip and cut out
seat, 6 sides, and 4 cross
pieces. Cut 4 legs from
squared strip to the
lengths shown.

2 ~ Stain pieces as
desired.

3 ~ Position seat about
halfway down and glue
to the back legs and the
tops of the front legs.

4 ~ Glue 4 side pieces
in between legs under
seat. Glue 2 side pieces
as slats between back
legs. Glue cross pieces
near bottom of legs.

**Chair seat
Cut 1**

**Back leg
Cut 2**

**Side piece
Cut 6**

**Front leg
Cut 2**

**Cross piece
Cut 4**